Susan Mitchell was born in Adelaide and began her career as a high
school teacher there in 1966. After teaching in London and travelling
around Europe, she returned to the University of South Australia,
where she is a senior lecturer in Communications. She teaches creative
writing and scriptwriting for radio and television. She has worked as a
cocktail waitress, a scriptwriter, a television presenter and a film extra.
She is currently presenting her own interview program, 'Susan
Mitchell: In Conversation', on ABC television. Her best-selling books
include *Tall Poppies, The Matriarchs, Winning Women, Tall Poppies
Too* and *Hot Shots*, her first novel.

PUBLIC LIVES
Private
Passions

Nine women talk about their lives and
their partnerships with influential men

Susan Mitchell

SIMON & SCHUSTER
AUSTRALIA

PUBLIC LIVES, PRIVATE PASSIONS

First published in Australasia in 1994 by
Simon & Schuster Australia
20 Barcoo Street, East Roseville NSW 2069

A Paramount Communications Company
Sydney New York London Toronto Tokyo Singapore

© 1994 Susan Mitchell

All rights reserved. No part of this publication may be reproduced, stored in a retrieval system, or transmitted, in any form or by any means, electronic, mechanical, photocopying, recording or otherwise, without the prior permission of the publisher in writing.

National Library of Australia
Cataloguing in Publication data

Mitchell, Susan, 1945–.
Public lives, private passions.

ISBN 0 7318 0391 4.

1. Women—Australia—Interviews. 2. Spouses—Australia—Interviews. 3. Celebrities—Australia. 4. Power (Social sciences). I. Title.

305.420994

Designed and typeset by Samphire Publishing Partners
Printed in Australia by Australian Print Group

To Richard

'A woman must no longer choose the role of the woman behind the great man, mother, sister, lover or wife to his genius. She must stop being the muse and become mistress of her own art, her own science, herself.'

Rebecca West, *The Freewoman,* 1911

'What I want is a strange conjunction ... not meeting and mingling, but an equilibrium, a pure balance of two single beings as the stars balance each other.'

D. H. Lawrence, *Women In Love,* 1921

Acknowledgments

Special thanks must go to the following: the University of South Australia; the management of former Australian Airlines, in particular, Barbara Stewart; my family, friends and colleagues for their suggestions and help; all the women who helped with the transcribing and typing; Kirsty Melville and Susan Morris-Yates from Simon & Schuster Australia; and, of course, to all the women in the book for their honesty and courage, and Mary Beasley, who never lets me give up.

Contents

Introduction

When my agent rang to ask me if I'd like to write a book on 'Women who live with powerful men', my initial reaction was, 'Why would I want to do that?' All of my previous books have been about women who attain power for themselves, not women who sit beside or stand behind it.

And then I saw Hillary Rodham Clinton on television, talking about not only having an equal partnership with the most powerful and influential man in the world, but acting on it. Hillary Clinton pushed out the boundaries that have always surrounded First Ladies. Her strong identification with working women and her sense of her own marriage as a real partnership had very positive spin-offs for all women. Hillary Clinton made public what many women were only passionate about in private. Gloria Steinem told the *New York Times*, 'She's pioneering in public an issue that is at least as important in the long term as any of the issues considered political in the conventional sense, and that issue is the equal relationship between a man and a woman.'

Prior to Hillary Clinton we were given the model of the woman 'behind every great man'. And yet so often those who preached this line were the very ones subverting it. Nancy Reagan camouflaged her campaigns to influence policy in the White House. Her devoted gaze and smiling adoration were a smokescreen for a manipulative woman who wielded enormous power behind the scenes. Marilyn Quayle stood on a platform that stated the need for mothers to stay at home while working daily from an office in the executive wing of the White House. The reality is that today most women are in two-income families and their major challenge is achieving an equal relationship and dual responsibility for parenting.

Hillary Clinton marked out her ground from the beginning of

her partnership with Bill. She backed his aspirations to become President to the hilt, but not at the expense of her own career. She is ranked among the top one hundred lawyers in the USA. She always took her responsibility as a parent seriously but expected him to do the same. When their daughter Chelsea was recently sick at school she told the teacher to ring her father because he would not be so hard to get. They view the family unit as a team where all the members are important. In an equal partnership, each helps the other according to the situation.

In the 1990s most women are engaged in this form of negotiation, a drawing up of equal territory. Often, especially if the man has a high profile or is successful and powerful, the woman is expected to take the back seat. If every woman wants her partner to be successful in what he chooses to do, regardless of whether he is a prime minister or a plumber, so too should every man want that for his partner. Too often the woman's career and aspirations are sacrificed for those of the man or the family. For too long women have colluded in this sacrifice.

How often do you hear women saying, 'I'm lucky because he does help with the dishes, or the housework, or the children'? The real question is, how much does he help and why should you feel lucky or grateful if what is offered is a fair contribution to an equal partnership?

With feminism, women have taken on the notion of choice. But choice involves change, and change is very often threatening. In the late twentieth century, when so many things have changed, we are being told that we are in 'the age of redefinition'. Nowhere has this redefinition been more radical or produced more heated debate than in the area of marriage or partnership between men and women. This book strives to put the issue firmly on the public agenda.

New definitions like 'equal partnerships', if they are to have any real meaning, must be matched by changes in individual behaviour. If you want to be treated like an equal then you must act like an equal. In order to act like an equal you must view yourself in that way, and in order to achieve it you must have a life that is yours apart from your partner and family. You must have a strong sense of yourself which is based on a healthy level of self-esteem. In this world of self-help books and instant questionnaires, you will need to give honest answers to questions like the following, if you wish to achieve an equal partnership.

• Do you believe that what you do is as important as what your partner does, regardless of how much money is earned?

• If the children are sick and you both work, do you take equal days off to look after them?

• If you really believed in something, how far would you go against your partner's wishes?

• Are you prepared to fight for an equal partnership?

• If the partnership is not equal and will never be, will you leave it?

• Do you determine how much you give and gain from the relationship?

• If you could have the relationship your heart desired, would it be the one you're in?

When we experience changes in our lives that do redefine who we are and how we are going to live, those changes will almost always produce a degree of anxiety. *It is stressful* to rethink and redefine who we are and what we want.

There are still women, many of them young women, who feel threatened by the notion of having a life that is separate from the one shared by partner and family. They are genuinely scared to assert their own needs and challenge the status quo in case they lose what they already have. Many women settle for less than they deserve from fear of loneliness, only to be left alone or widowed with no real sense of themselves and no resources to develop it. A life delayed is a life half-lived. But there are an increasing number of women who will no longer settle for an unequal relationship. Economic independence has given them a sense of choice, a sense of not settling for less. They refuse to stay in relationships where their needs are seen as peripheral. In order to achieve equality in relationships, it is women who have challenged the status quo. Many men are still threatened and resistant to such challenges, but if they are to achieve full, satisfying and equal relationships with women, they, too, will have to change.

For too long many women have led public lives that have buried or hidden their private passions. Uppermost in these desires or passions has been a deeply felt need to pursue some talent of their own. Too often women have allowed themselves to view these private passions as selfish needs. Rebecca West, that brilliant writer in the first wave of feminism, attacked the feminine ideal of self-sacrifice as dangerous and reactionary. She said it was a sin against life itself. She roused women to do battle with their own masochism to weed out the natural slave, the victim in their souls.

There is still no point in assuming the role of victim and attempting to blame your husband or your family or yourself—blame is a totally wasteful and destructive emotion. If you really want to achieve equality, you have to take responsibility for the situation in which you find yourself, and act. You have to participate actively in change and adjust the patterns of behaviour that govern your life.

The women in this book are involved in partnerships with publicly successful and powerful men in a wide range of professions. Many of these women were reluctant to be interviewed, because so often other people had said they wanted to talk to them as a ruse to gain information about their partners. Some of them have had celebrity status conferred on them because of the activities of their partners. My aim was to reveal the nature of the relationship, to discover whether they were equal partners or whether the power in the relationship changed according to changing circumstances. I attempted to discover the private passions that pulsed beneath the skin of their public lives.

To peel back the public mask and strip away the gloss of celebrity is never easy. Of course, they did not tell me everything; some interviews took longer than others, but I have used them as the starting point to think about the essential truth of most women's lives.

What emerged was a documentary of each woman's attempt to make sense of her life and her relationship with her partner. This book is a living history of a wide range of women's relationships with men, covering most of the twentieth century. The fact that their partners are sometimes famous or powerful, or both, only serves to highlight the basic issues being explored. Because these women have linked their lives with men who are influential, the pressure on them to allow their own needs, their private passions, to be subsumed by their public lives has sometimes been very strong. Some have resisted better than others. Equality should not depend on the occupation of either partner.

All women will identify with these women's struggles to love their partners, to be supportive and helpful, to be good partners or mothers and, perhaps even more importantly, to find their own identity—to develop and maintain that sense of self in order to establish an equal partnership.

Why should any of us settle for less?

Discovering the Self

Helen Gibson

Eileen Bond

Betty Churcher

Part I   Discovering the Self

Helen Gibson and Eileen Bond were highly spirited, bright and adventurous, and by marrying young felt they were escaping from the straitjacket of their schools, their parents and their society. Betty Churcher escaped not into marriage, but overseas in order to free herself from the expectations of a conformist and repressive Victorian upbringing.

Helen Gibson and Eileen Bond married their first real boyfriends, having never worked at anything they liked. Betty Churcher was very sure about where her talent and her passion lay, but was not sure how she could go about developing it. Even though she married another artist, she was determined to continue with her own work. When she had children, however, she made the conscious choice to put her energies into being a mother. During this period her partner's career flourished while hers remained stagnant.

While Helen Gibson and Eileen Bond allowed their own lives to merge into those of their husbands or their children, Betty Churcher never lost sight of her own need to fulfil her potential.

To have a passion is to pursue something that you love as an extension of yourself and your own identity. Betty found a way of combining her public life with her private passion. When the personal and the professional merge, the discovery of self is exhilarating.

Helen Gibson

Not many people had heard of Helen Gibson prior to the public break-up of her long marriage to Mike Gibson. In his regular column in the *Women's Weekly*, Mike often referred to his child bride and his five children. His tongue-in-cheek column was about good old-fashioned family values from the point of view of the beleaguered breadwinner.

Gibbo had worked his way to the top in both radio and television and the culmination of his success was a multi-million-dollar contract as a television host. Just when it looked as if he was a man who had it all, he left his wife and his family.

In my mind I had characterised it as another male story of fame, money, mid-life crisis, during which the old model is traded in for the new—new wife, new lifestyle. I didn't know Helen Gibson and had prepared myself to meet a bitter, rejected woman full of regrets and resentment about what had happened to her. Instead, the woman who opened the door was cheerful, open and honest, with not a trace of self-pity or bitterness. We sat in the living room of her modest house and she talked to me as someone whose life was still ahead of her.

I was fourteen when I first met Mike Gibson. I don't think I thought about what I wanted to do. I didn't know who I was. Unless you have an absolute goal, like 'I want to be a doctor', or 'I want to go to Africa and save souls; I want to be a missionary', unless you are absolutely dedicated to what you want to do, at the age of fourteen I think you just want to escape the wrath of your teachers. I find that my daughters are just finding out now, in their twenties, what they actually want to do.

My father died when I was ten. He was in the air force during the war and he had a massive heart attack and lived on for another two years, but there was no open-heart surgery in those days so he was expected to live two years and that was exactly how long he lasted. There was just my mum and myself, because I was an only child. I didn't go to a private school and Mum had a bit of a battle. Years ago women weren't really looked after either, in that situation. Luckily my father had taken out a super fund and he'd had quite a big job. We lived in London for a few years where he worked at Australia House trying to get all the disgruntled Poms over here. This was the early Fifties. I was born in 1944. Mum basically did housework. They offered her a small pension or a lump sum which would have been enough just to buy a house. She took the pension, which is indexed, and has lived quite well on it.

I got on reasonably well with my mother. I am much more like my father—he was much more aggressive and demanding of life than my mum—but I never really knew him. My memories of him are all horrible because he was not a good patient when he was sick, and he used to throw things at me. He had remarkable range and very good eyes. I went to Cremorne High and met Michael when I was there. He had been to City Boys the previous year and was in his first year of law.

I was waiting at Neutral Bay tram stop to go home to Lane Cove. It was a Sunday night and I had just been to confirmation classes—I did this as something to do, because I was never terribly churchy. I had a friend who was going to do it with me. A mutual friend, a guy that I knew, and Michael stopped and we had a chat. And then I think he called. I had a lot of male friends, which was unusual in those days for girls. I preferred male company to women. Maybe I had two or three really close girlfriends at that age, but I was never a great one for women. At school I used to think they were stupid sitting there in their lunch hours working out what their wedding dress would look like, actually doing drawings of it. Or  they'd sit around working out what names they'd call their children. I didn't know what I wanted to do but it certainly wasn't all that rubbish. Yet I was the first to be married. I always preferred male company, but I never had a boyfriend as such. The odd boy walked me home occasionally. Michael was the first boyfriend.

We just spent all our time together, and when I was about sixteen we wanted to get married. Our parents put up a terrible scene, as you can imagine.

I was madly in love—not just the physical attraction, but I had never met anyone whose brain worked the same way mine did. We really hit it off. I was always rebellious at school and I was supposedly brilliant but never applied myself. I was so brilliant that I fought it, which is really dumb, basically. I felt I knew everything, and of course at fourteen you know nothing. I left school when I was fourteen and three months, and my mother allowed me to leave on condition that I did something. I did hairdressing, which I hated. I was good at it, but I could never work out why women would spend so much time worrying about their hair, which is not a good way for a hairdresser to feel—it should have been the centre of my life. I was not emotionally equipped to deal with women who were having nervous breakdowns because this side of their hair wasn't the same as this side. That was at the time when hairdos were at the side and you couldn't sweep one side over; it all had to look exactly the same. Like those Japanese Mikado ladies—it shouldn't look like hair, but something you had put on your head. Hairdressing and I were not compatible.

When I first met Michael I used to take sickies from school and then from work. By then he was into newspapers; he'd given law away because he realised that Perry Mason wasn't quite the same as real life. Newspapers are much more like the real world and he used to cover the races and dogs. So he'd be going down to a race meeting and I'd nick off and get the train down there. When I was sixteen we made a fuss about getting married and then we threatened all sorts of terrible things, like running away God-knows-where. Finally they gave in, which amazed us both. So we got married. We had nothing, absolutely nothing. My mum used to feed us on a Wednesday night because Thursday was payday. This was during the recession—1960, 1961—there were no jobs for hairdressers, and I couldn't get work. So we were just living on his salary, which was fifteen pounds a week. We paid eight guineas a week rent. I nearly went crazy all day. It was terrible. When I think back on all the yucky places we lived—horrid! We lived in a place at Mosman, which now has been turned into the most magnificent town houses, which are now something like $800 000 each. At that stage it was a series of rooms and you all shared the kitchen and the bathroom. I couldn't cook. The first chicken I cooked I left the giblets inside a plastic bag. All the plastic melted—it was a total disaster. Then I remember another year when I cooked a rabbit, and I must have bought it cheap because it still had a lot of fluff on it. I had started to casserole it and didn't realise that cornflour doesn't thicken until it reaches boiling point, so I kept adding more and more, and finally it all thickened and the rabbit was stuck in the pot, and wouldn't come out because it was stuck in this glue.

We were extremely happy, but things were a bit rough. After about four years Michael had the chance to go to London for the football tour. It was a real long one, about four and a half months. We thought I'd stay here and he'd go over there, and we'd see what happened. Nothing was really discussed, because you didn't talk about things in those days. So off he went. He used to write every day. If I didn't get seven notes a week I'd think he was sick. We were best friends and romantic. You can't beat it. That's the killer, when you've had it and it goes. You can never find it again. You lose your lover and your best friend. After it's gone, it's gone. I suppose that's life, but in a way you wouldn't want something else to come and replace that. It can never be the same because you're different. You're not young and generous with all these expectations of life. You've been there and done that—I suppose jaded is the wrong word but you are a little, even if you try not to be. It's just natural.

Anyhow, in London Mike was told, 'You're doing such a

good job and someone is coming home. How about you stay in London and do sport and general features?' This was the London office of ACP, which was the *Telegraph*, the *Weekly* and I think they had *Weekend*. When he started at the office they said, 'How about we bring your wife over?'

I was twenty when I arrived in London. We decided to have a child and I had my first baby. In a way it was very lonely, and a very scary experience for me, because I knew nothing about children. I had never even had a nephew or a niece. Being from a very small family, I didn't know what it was like to hold a baby until I held my own. It was scary, but I was full of confidence. She was born over there, and then after four months we decided we'd had enough. By that stage we were very settled in our relationship and we used to feel very sorry for friends who split up and got divorced. We both thought that we would never break up; it was something that happened to other people.

I did work in London before I had the baby, part-time hairdressing there. I used to try and send some money back home so that at least we would have something, but we were still broke when we got back. Journalists were pretty poorly paid, but Mike loved it.

We were very happy and I was very contented. At that stage there was nothing else I wanted to pursue. And then I fell pregnant again. There is only fifteen months between the girls. Actually, the way I fell pregnant was really quite funny. At that stage I was on the Pill, and one week we played cards at our place and we lost, and we were so broke I couldn't afford to buy the Pill.

I still had no desire to work. I didn't get the desire until the children were off my hands when I went back just part-time to hairdressing again. But I still hated it.

I used to do a lot with Michael. I was a real media freak. I'd help him with research and newspaper clippings, especially when he was on radio. It got really busy when he was at the top in radio because it was really at its peak. In the Seventies we'd be out four or five nights a week. And it was very difficult. Luckily I had a very good baby-sitter.

I can't speak on Michael's behalf about being faithful. There may have been an occasional woman, perhaps, when he went overseas, but it is not something that I ever mulled over or questioned him about. I think he was faithful and I was very faithful. I still am.

I knew he could find someone else, but we were so compatible that I never felt threatened. We became in a way one person, which is not good. And I was the one who got lost, while Michael was the one always up front. Even though it was never deliberate on his part, nor did I want it to be any other way, in retrospect it was probably not a good thing. If I had my time over again I would pursue something different from him.

After five kids, life went on much the same, but we got richer. I remember when Mike signed with Packer to do a daily sports column, they actually paid him $200 a week. That was a fortune. The average wage then was something like $80. We thought we'd never have to worry about money again, and then of course about four years down the track it started to not look so good. As long as you stick with newspapers and magazines you are never going to be rich. You associate with a lot of rich people, and you might have a lot of rich friends, but you are never going to be the rich one.

Radio was a totally different thing, because it only takes about eighty people to produce 24-hour-a-day radio. They get advertising in for roughly the same price as TV and are churning this product out with a huge profit. That's when the salaries were even bigger than television. Television started to get bigger and take over when the Loweys bought Channel 10 because they didn't know a lot about television but they had a lot of money. They thought, 'If we can just buy the names we will be right'. They were wonderful people, always ready to take a chance, and they were the ones who actually set the wage standard of the time. This is the early Eighties. Once they set the standard everyone else had to try and keep up, and in lots of ways that's what brought TV to its knees—too much money going out and not enough revenue coming in.

Michael was away for long periods of time, like for the Commonwealth Games. Even in the early days when I had three young children, he was still doing football tours. He left when Kate was four days old and came back when she was nearly crawling. I just thought the kids were my responsibility, and I certainly didn't resent it. He was out working and I was the home person. I was quite happy with the way it was. It got very heavy going when we had a lot of teenagers, especially girls; I don't think I worried more than Michael, but I still worried. Waiting up can cause friction in a marriage.

The children were the only reason we argued. Having five kids used to put us into a frame of mind where we would argue, which could lead to bad feelings and then bad feelings would come out as something else. We would probably never have had an argument if it hadn't been for the children. In all our years in London I can't remember us having a fight—ever. Now that's amazing. There were no in-laws, no children, no influences. Basically we got angry about things that are external. Like, you've had a really bad day at work and you come home and you take it out on those you care about most, which is just dreadful. It's easier to go home and kick the cat than go to the gym and work it off before you go home.

When Michael was very well paid, nothing in our lives really changed. We always had a bucket of money on top of the fridge and the kids still talk about it, because once there was nothing left in there, everyone went without. Even the time we had no money, the routine was the same. I would go to the bank and take out so much money and throw it in the bucket. I handled everything. Women, being women, do have a

weakness for certain things that tend to be expensive, and I suppose if you've got a bit of money you indulge it. I always loved old jewellery, and every Christmas and birthday Mike would buy me something really nice in that line. I was a little spoilt in that, but I think basically when Mike earned really big money our life didn't change. He wouldn't buy stupid expensive vehicles to drive around in; he was more of a Scot than I am. As long as he had a pair of clean jeans, a clean pair of shorts and a T-shirt, he'd be happy. He was never one to be swayed by money.

I don't really know what went wrong with our marriage. I

had a lot of emotional problems. I think that being married so young, I had never really found myself. If you've never found yourself, how can you ever have a proper relationship? Because you don't really know who you are. I still don't know who I really am. It's curious.

I suddenly came to the conclusion that I wasn't suited to marriage. After about twenty-eight years of it, it suddenly occurred to me, when I looked back, 'What am I doing all this for? I don't really want to live like this.' It was my mid-life crisis. Michael wanted his happy, wonderful, together person back, and what he had was this angry, horrible bitch. I can't blame him for leaving me. I did at the time, but looking back now, I think I would have left me. I love him still.

I realised that I wasn't cut out for motherhood and being a wife. I think I'm just a slow learner.

It all came together—my drinking, my health, his male menopause. I totally understand that there comes a point in a man's life when, having worked hard since he was eighteen, he realises when he's fifty that his life is the best it's ever going to get. Every field in the media Michael had gone into he had ended up number one. When he had finally made it to the big time the kids seemed to be always getting to him and asking him for money. I'm sure he felt that, combined with my attitude at that time, he was just being used. He wanted some happiness out of it all, which is fair enough. Not too much to ask.

So Mike found someone else who was bright and happy, the attitude he liked. Maybe if she hadn't been around I think we probably would have worked things out. For the first time in our lives we didn't talk. He just seemed to get terribly angry with me. We could have worked on it, but we didn't seem to know where to start, as it was a problem we had never confronted before. We had always talked about everything. I didn't know what was wrong with me, and he didn't know what was wrong with me, so it was a real mess. We just got further and further away from each other.

It was like, 'I've got a lost ticket here but I don't know where to hand it in.' It's wonderful now, because I have the freedom that I've never had in my life. I went from my mother, saying to me at the age of sixteen, 'Where have you been?' and 'You're lazy', to being a wife with responsibilities to a husband, to being a mother myself. I was an excellent wife; I was always there. I even cut his damned hair. I did everything. But I lost sight of other things. Eventually I wasn't even interested in sex and was just a shit. The point is, I didn't know why. If you had given me a million dollars I couldn't have given you the reasons. It just crept up on me and even the children didn't notice. I know I'm obsessive. If I clean the kitchen I don't want anyone to muck up my kitchen. That's the sort of person who shouldn't live with someone. I took my anger out on the children and Michael.

I was devastated when Michael left. It was terrible. Because we had become one, it was just like losing a leg. Like suddenly being crippled. In reality you are crippled emotionally, because you then think, 'Have I ever had an original thought in my life? Have I ever thought for myself? What did I think about when I was thirteen and a half? What did I get for my fourteenth birthday?' I suddenly realised that I had never known myself. I also developed a massive problem with drinking, as a result of my emotional problems. It crept up on me, ready to grab me at my weakest. My life was full: full of kids, full of their friends, full of Michael's friends. Not my friends. They were all mutual friends, as we'd been together since the age of fourteen. If you get married later, I think you hang on to your girlfriends.

After the split, I had to pull myself together. I nearly died.

My liver packed up because of the booze, but also I found out I had a liver weakness which I'd probably had from birth. What I was drinking probably wasn't all that bad, but it had the same effect on me as someone who was drinking a bottle and a half of Scotch a day. I'd have about eight or nine glasses of wine a day, which would have the same effect on me, but wouldn't be regarded in alcoholic terms as being massive. As somebody said to me, 'Gawd, that would be just for starters before breakfast for me'. But I was dependent on it, and it nearly destroyed me. I thought, 'I'm not going to get out of this. I can't argue my way out of it, my liver won't listen to me.' So I went into therapy for several weeks—it was therapy for drinking, I suppose, but drinking wasn't really my problem, I was my problem. Once I managed to sort myself out, I haven't had a drink. AA was great for me. For some people it is hard and I believe it. I've seen some people at AA meetings and they are tearing out their hair. I still go there. I'm not going to let that go, because you can't afford to be complacent and I respect the fact that I'll never be cured. I haven't found giving up drinking hard. The big test will be when I'm facing a real crisis, like a death in the family. I go to AA two or three times a week. Some days I don't want to go but I push myself. I know I've still got a long way to go.

You've got to start feeling good about yourself, because what hits rock bottom is your self-esteem. It just goes out the window. And you really have to work hard at building it. Only other people with the same problem can help you. That's why AA works so well.

I'd been drinking over the limit probably for about ten years. It had nothing to do with my marriage break-up. Drink didn't really change me. I think it made me a nicer, warmer person, easier to get along with.

When I was in hospital, I was very depressed. I really didn't know what I was doing. I was all over the place. I was doing stupid things, just trying to escape. I was trying to find something, but I didn't understand that what I had to find was me. Michael and I did not talk after the break-up. I was hurt. I was angry. The kids were growing up. We had planned our life. Mike was going to semi-retire, do a bit of travel writing. It was going to be wonderful. Suddenly there was nothing—no Michael, no future, no plans.

I got the impression that someone else was waiting for him, because he had never ever left me. Except once. It was one of those stupid things. He had packed up a few things and decided he would go up to the local hotel. When he was halfway over there he realised he didn't have any money so he came back, knocked at the front door very humbly. He was gone for about ten minutes.

In the early stages I was so sick I didn't care about the fact that he'd gone. A friend spoke to me who had gone through the same thing, but she dug her heels in and she fought. And she said, 'Why didn't you do that?' I was too sick and too mentally exhausted. I just wanted to die.

I always thought therapy was shit. I thought anyone who has to go and see a shrink has got a certain lack of balls, because they can't sort out their own problems. And like everybody who feels that way, I thought I didn't have a problem. The world had a problem, I didn't. The world wouldn't fit in with me.

I think I showed my anger in really bizarre ways. I used to get cranky when Mike and I had to go out to functions. He was always wonderful, he would never just walk off and leave me. I wasn't a total dill. I think sometimes he would just worry about walking away instead of worrying about what I might say to people. I could always put on a facade of being terribly confident. I remember this terribly pompous man who was sitting between Mike and me. He was devoting the whole night to talking to Michael and then I think he must have felt a bit uncomfortable because he hadn't even acknowledged my existence. He said, 'And what do you do, dear?' I said, 'I drink.' And he said something like, 'Oh, that's nice.' He wasn't even listening. I could have said, 'Well, I go out and murder my mother and then when I'm really bored I strangle old ladies and—' I could have said anything and he would have said, 'Oh, that's nice.'

I was the appendage. I like to think it didn't worry me, but underneath it must have unconsciously. I was clearly thinking, 'I'm a person', but then I'd think to myself, 'Well, what sort of person are you? Do you really know?' I had therapy for seven weeks. At St Edmund's Hospital. Some people are there for three weeks, some for two days—it just depends. A sign out the front says something about 'for the emotionally disturbed'. It's on a very busy road and some days when I was particularly bored, a person who became a friend when we were there together, we would go out and pull weird faces at the motorists going past. They would all just look. It was a scream. The staff at the hospital were just wonderful. They don't teach you anything. I don't know the secret, but you reveal things to yourself. You talk in groups and it opens up your mind to really stand back and look at yourself. You have this flash. I saw an AA movie on it and you see people covered with this golden haze and it looks wonderful. We all used to joke about it. Someone would say, 'What are you doing?' And I'd reply, 'Oh, I'm bored, just sitting here waiting for the golden haze.' It was really just like being struck by lightning. And I thought, 'How did I not see this?' It was so simple.

I never drank a lot whilst I was out; I would drink at home. Women do that. At home no-one is tested for a liquor problem. When I was well I had tests done for blood and sugar, diabetes and everything. Nobody ever thought about testing my liver. I was just off colour, and then suddenly one day I turned yellow. They really thought that I had liver cancer or a massive liver blockage.

My liver is still causing me problems. Even if I never have another drink—which I won't. I can't because I'll die. I don't think about dying, because there's no point in living another thirty years and spending every single day thinking this might be your last.

I'm now looking at what I want to do with the rest of my life, and it doesn't involve getting married again or being involved with anyone.

I'm not a terribly passionate person. Passion is different from obsession, and I get obsessions. I had a hat obsession; if you were to go through my house you would see hats hanging off the wall everywhere. That lasted about eighteen months. Then when I got glasses I got an obsession about frames, and I couldn't walk past an optician without going in and buying some. Then I went through my hand-painting stage. I painted the dining room table. Then I did murals on the walls, but they looked horrible so I painted them over again. I'm dabbling with a lot of things that I haven't had time to do, trying to find something to do well. It could take a long while. I know some things I'm hopeless at, so I rule them out totally, but I'm the sort of person who wants to pursue something and get it right.

I'm not like that now, but I was obsessive as a cleaner. If I had to leave the house at nine o'clock I would do as much housework before nine o'clock as I would do during the day I wasn't going out. I would get up at six o'clock and start. I couldn't leave that house with a toy on the floor or a piece of dirty clothing left on the bed. That's obsessive. They're all bad signs. Someone who has those emotional problems is obviously going to carry them through into other things. It's the disease of the perfectionist. I started to feel I wasn't measuring up and I wasn't as perfect as I thought I was. I started to really disappoint myself. It's clearly a sign of low self-esteem.

Michael and I are now back to being good friends. That's as good as I want. For some reason, marriage is just not good for me. I think it destroyed me, or I allowed it to destroy me. It will take me some time to rebuild myself.

For me to live in a relationship now, I can't even imagine the man he would have to be. A person who never ate, who never got his clothes dirty, who was content to sleep in another room so I could have the whole bed to myself, but be an attentive lover on command and also take me out to meals. I haven't seen too many men like that. I think they are a bit short on the ground, and my demands are a bit expensive.

My nature is such that I tend to submerge myself in whatever I'm doing. That is why I have five kids rather than one or two, why I have at least thirty hats when I've only got one head. People find it very hard to put up with me. I would be terrible to live with. I wouldn't inflict that on anyone.

I'm thinking of doing counselling for mature age students, mostly because I got so much from it and I was so against it. I had to nearly die before even giving it a chance. I didn't hold out very much hope at all. Having been in a coma and somehow got out of it, I think I've really got to make something out of the rest of my life. When I came out of the coma I could not talk properly; my memory was gone totally. All I could remember was my name and my children's names. I couldn't remember the street I lived in or the number. I could imagine where I lived, I could see the street, but I couldn't put a name to it. I couldn't remember any friends—but then I remembered one and thought, 'I must be a bitch; I have only one friend.'

I really thought I had blown my own mind, but then after about two days things started coming back. Not everything immediately, but there were things I couldn't remember like my phone number. Now, the last letters of my phone number make the year my son was born, and I always thought that was funny when I moved here, to get that number. I couldn't remember it. It is just unbelievable what you can do to yourself. It's scary.

I think I'm a good mother. I don't think I'm a terribly nice mother, not as mothers should be. Savannah tells the story of when she was in about fifth class—she was about ten—and there was this horrible girl in her class telling this story about me, that I was a prostitute because I wore crazy earrings and wore funny clothes and I dyed my hair red. I didn't act like a mother, play tennis three days a week—I didn't turn up at school with streaked hair looking wonderful.

Not so long ago I was in Fiji and my son Danny and I were on the beach and he saw my tattoos. He said, 'I always thought good mothers don't do this. Good mothers don't have tattoos.' I have had my tattoo three years. I had always wanted one. I got it just after Mike left. I have two on my back. I must stop having them, but I keep thinking, 'I'll just have one more.' That's probably how I started drinking. 'I'll just have one more.' I'm a person who can get addicted to things very easily.

When Michael left, it seemed like the end of the world. After bringing up one son and four girls, of course we had all had our minor dramas and weren't all squeaky clean, but we were a close family. We all thought we would never survive the break-up, but we did. The kids are all really good friends with each other, which is important to me.

I had convinced myself I couldn't live without Michael. I don't think it any more. It wasn't me married to him all those years. It was me conforming. It's not that I want to go around the streets with nothing on, shouting obscenities. But I feel now I'm in charge of my own life, and whatever I do wrong, there's only me to blame, and whenever I do right, I'm responsible for that as well.

I don't think what happened to me has anything to do with becoming rich and famous. External things don't affect a relationship, certainly not ours. I would have deflated Mike if he had become big-headed. At one stage he bought himself a Mazda RX–7. And I made jokes that he'd start wearing one of those funny hats and have all his chest hair hanging out of his shirt and rattle with gold chains. I was even making jokes at the car sales place when we went to pick up the car. He had to finally get rid of it because it kept getting stolen. Probably by someone who wanted to look like that.

Once you've been married for any length of time, you know each other so intimately. Once you know someone's bowel habits there's not much illusion left, is there? You can't go on role playing through a marriage. One partner will just say, 'Hang on, who is this talking?' There was never any danger of him getting carried away with his media image.

I avoided the celebrity bit like the plague. I always hid. I hated all that. I can see it's necessary and some people enjoy it, and that's fine; it's just not me. If I absolutely had to go to something I would go along and always be pleasant. I wouldn't be offensive to anyone. I'd always try to enter into it to a degree, but it wasn't really Michael either. He's not terribly gregarious. Anyone on television is a role player. The funniest people on stage are often the most boring people you could ever live with. I used to feel sorry for Michael, because people assumed that because he wrote about sports that's all he wanted to talk about. They'd never stop going on to him about sport—but that all goes with the territory, and you put up with it. People think that what they see is the reality. And of course that's not true. The 'him' that presents itself to the world is totally different to the 'him' at home.

The women's movement came along when I had five children. I still don't approve of a lot of it, and yet in other ways I think they haven't gone far enough, or they've done it the wrong way. People are now so confused about their roles that you wonder whether it's all worthwhile.

One of the reasons many women were put off was that most of the women were academics. It basically started off at university. They'd cross the road when they saw me coming, and I probably had better thoughts about the movement than they did. Michael and I had the kind of relationship where he couldn't wait to come home to me to tell me what had happened during the day. And that's the best kind of relationship. We shared everything. It was good, but it wasn't enough. It stopped being enough when the children started to grow up and there was nothing left for me to do. I decided after the fifth child, for my own sake and my own health, that I should have something radical done about it. I was going to get my tubes tied and then I thought, 'No, blow this, he can go and have a bit of surgery; I'll make him suffer.' He wasn't too happy for a couple of weeks after the operation. He walked around looking as if he'd just fallen off a horse. Men do carry on about things.

When you have five kids it really is hard to juggle everything. He was never good with babies and not very good with teenagers, but he was excellent when they were between the ages of two and seven, great at telling bedtime stories, taking them to the park.

I was always seen as the person who was totally in control. When the children were very young, our house had to be run like an army barracks. Clothes had to be laid out the night before for school. I was brilliant. I really was. I had friends who used to ring me and say they were really feeling down because they weren't coping and they had only two children. I made them realise that their workload wasn't quite what they thought, because I could handle five and do it in such a way as to make it look easy. But as the children got older, I couldn't handle it, there would be obstacles thrown into my path and that would blow my system. Once my system was blown I was like a computer in which somebody had pushed the wrong button; everything would go crazy. And that's when I started to think, 'I'm not handling life very well.' That's probably when I started having a problem with drinking.

I had two shifts with cooking. When the kids were very young, I'd feed them early and then when they got older we'd all eat together. Then of course it got to the stage when we'd never all eat together because people were coming and going at various times. Mike and I pretty well shared a meal every night.

We had a good life together, and I don't regret it. When the kids got off to school it was such a relief after having them around all the time. That's when I should have started pursuing a career. Stupidly, I didn't. I looked at the reorganisation, all the reprogramming that would have been necessary, and it all became a bit much. I decided against it.

All the kids are great now and doing well in their chosen careers. So it's time for me to get my own act together.

I'm into framing, at the moment, teaching myself how to do mounts. My bedroom looks like a very bad art gallery. Obviously what I've got to do is throw myself into something worthwhile, because I know what I'm like. I've even learned to tone down my hair. When I have red hair it looks like a carrot. I'm learning to be more subdued, because I've got nothing to prove. It's all an adventure now, at least that's how I like to think of it. Anything's possible.

Helen told me to walk to the end of the narrow street that her house was in, as taxis could never find it.

'It's not like our old home in Cremorne. You know, it was valued at $1.2 million before we split up, but by the time we sold it the market had dropped and we only got three-quarters of a million. That's a lot of money to kiss goodbye. I said to Mike recently, "You've got no sense of timing. You could have waited till the market improved to pack your bags."'

She laughs and there's not a trace of bitterness in it. It's the laugh of someone who knows that what she's got now is far more precious to her than money.

Eileen Bond

It was fortunate that not only Eileen Bond but also her secretary, Sue Park, had read my previous books. Sue was my best advocate in achieving the interview. At one stage it seemed impossible that Eileen Bond would be in the country at a time when I could fly to Perth. I was about to abandon the task when one last phone call to Sue made one Friday a possibility. I booked a ticket and said I would be there no matter what. At this stage I had never spoken to Eileen Bond.

On the plane journey I read Paul Barry's book, *The Rise and Fall of Alan Bond*. It was Alan Bond winning the America's Cup in 1983 that made him a national hero and put the spotlight on his wife, Eileen, the woman everyone called Red. By the end of that decade Alan Bond had fallen from grace and all the politicians who had flocked to shake his hand and drink his wine no longer wanted to know him.

Eileen was hardly mentioned in Barry's book, and when I met the author many months later he seemed amazed that she had agreed to talk to me. I said I had made it clear that I wanted to talk about her life, not her husband's, and had made a commitment not to talk about his business deals.

When I arrived at the house the gate was open and I walked up to the front door and rang the bell. I was shown into a study full of brown velvet couches, lined with books and warmed by an open fire.

Eileen arrived, shook my hand, sat down on the opposite couch and said, 'Sorry I wasn't there to greet you, but I got up late. I've got a lousy cold.'

She was nervous. Not, I suspected, about meeting me, but at the prospect of questions which she might not want to answer. I knew there was an agreed line over which I could not step. She did not call her restaurant Paparazzi without a sense of irony.

I was a terrific little girl. I was the youngest of five and my oldest brother would probably say I'm a spoilt brat even though we are very close. I had a great childhood.

I don't remember too much about dolls. It was adventurous living in Fremantle then, very different from how it is now. I was born around '38. We were right in the middle near St Patrick's Church. I used to walk to Sacred Heart School and many a time came home with my school uniform covered in mulberries from climbing trees.

We were a close family. We have all gone very different ways but have remained in close contact with each other. Whatever happens, I always know my family is there.

I came from an Irish Catholic background and I guess that influenced our lives a lot. I can probably sing any Irish song that was ever written—we all sang a lot. My father was very involved in Fremantle, especially local government. He was in the wool business.

The Irish are not totally sensible. My mother mostly sang songs. She died when she was sixty-two and my father didn't die until he was eighty-five. So my association was a lot longer with my father. It seems like my dad was always there. He would take me to high school in the car and all that sort of thing. We all thought we were his favourite. There were three girls and two boys. We had normal kids' quarrels. My oldest brother couldn't stand the sight of me because when he was going out on dates I'd ask him where he was going and drive him crazy.

I was married for a long time. When I first married Alan I was still growing up. I was outgoing. We were very young. It was the ultimate thing for a Catholic girl to do, get married and have kids.

When I was young I was busy having a good time; then I was married and having children and still having a good time. I think the best thing is being a mother. I still do.

I didn't like school much. The Irish nuns were very bossy. We were all brought up by them and had wonderful teaching, and when you had babies you went to St John of God Hospital. It was full of Irish nuns and they bossed you around and you were too frightened not to do exactly what they told you. I had an aunty who was a nun. You were so blessed if you had a nun or a priest in your family. We still think we are because my brother is a priest. My faith was integrated into my life. It was always there.

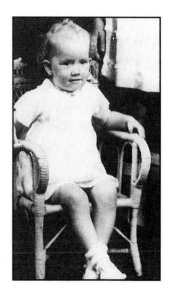

I met Alan ballroom dancing. My sister was a very good dancer and I went along with her. I thought he was a bit cheeky. But we got on pretty well, right from the start. I was seventeen and had left school and was thinking about where I would work and my father was thinking I shouldn't work. He thought it was quite nice for me to stay home, being the youngest. I did go to work in an office, but that was for a very small time. My father thought I could stay home and help my mother—that would be a very nice thing to do. There wasn't any rush to go out and do anything. Everybody else in the family was working, so I wasn't pressured into anything.

I would have married Alan if I was pregnant or not. You didn't have to worry about what to do, you just did it. In Catholic families you went to a Catholic doctor. It was what everybody did. I didn't mind being pregnant very young. I had three children in three years. I had no greater aspirations at that time of my life.

Alan worked like a demon, so therefore I spent a lot of time being with the children independent of Alan. My role was bringing up the children.

Alan was good fun—he was forward, but serious in what he was doing. I think I am a bit more fun-loving than Alan. I liked the role of being a mother; I liked the relationship with the children.

You did roll with the punches all those years ago. Married life was tough, and then all of a sudden you find you haven't done much except be at home and be married, and thank God you liked being a mother, because if you didn't life would have been a lot more difficult.

We started off living in a little apartment just out of Fremantle. I guess you would call it a flat, really. Part of a house. That was all great fun. We rented it. I was playing house. Alan worked damned hard and could make money. His passion was business. It wasn't even money, it was business. And that was how the flow of things went. He did one deal after another and I had one baby after the other.

We had great parents to help us. I always had my mum and dad, and my relations were always there. I could always go home if I wanted to. But having babies wasn't the only thing we did. Our life was just progressing at such a rate. Things were happening in business. We put the foundations of the house down. You could do that then. Put the foundations down and live in the garage, but it wasn't in fact a garage. It was a bedroom and a kitchen, and we built the house from there.

There was no time to sit around and think, 'What do I do next?'

I was a good housewife, although the first time I cooked a rabbit I left it with its arms and legs out. I knew nothing about cooking. I can remember Alan coming home and first of all smelling it and then I think it went out the window. We went to our parents' place and got fed.

I did learn to cook. But I was lucky to be surrounded by people we could go to. It all seems easy, talking to you now, but it wasn't so easy at the time.

From that house we went to another, bigger house. We sold it before it was finished. By the time Craig was born we were living in another area again.

Alan wasn't a Catholic; he became one. We had lovely times, exciting times and some awful times. He was always my best friend; he still is. I don't think in any marriage you only see good in someone. You see people in all their different ways, good and bad. Learning how to be a wife and mother wasn't easy. We were both just kids. We were the same age.

They were very happy children. Alan was a good parent, but the kids never knew where he was at any given time in their lives, so I took on the parenting role and took them to school, picked them up. I didn't have to work. How do people manage it nowadays, take on a full-time job with children? In a way it is tougher for them than it was for me. I didn't ever have to go out. I made sure I was there a lot because of the absences of Alan.

I always managed to do a hell of a lot, even when the children were small. Being president of the Ladies' Auxiliary at Aquinas College was a good start to my organisational ability and great fun—I remember organising the cocktail parties to raise money for a swimming pool. And the tuckshop—polony rolls were big on the menu ...

I clearly did things right, because we didn't have the pressures of having to go to work. I thought I was terrific at it. If you enjoy something I'm sure you're good at it. It's like if you're giving a party and having a good time, then you're sure everybody else is.

Like all normal kids, I argued about everything with them, but I always made the final decision. Alan and I didn't argue a lot. Maybe over the children occasionally. His being away a lot didn't worry me. You get into the habit of not having someone around and then it becomes quite simple not having to cater to someone all the time. I wouldn't recommend the separations to everybody. You do become a little bit too independent. We seemed to survive all that, and then fell down at the end, which was amazing.

Alan loves the excitement of things; I do a bit, too.

Alan came from a Church of England background, and when he came to live in Australia his father had been separated from him for a long time because of the war. So we did have differences. I had never been separated from my family at all.

Alan got on with my family. He was very unique. They had never seen anything like him. Alan would say or do anything. Strangely, my father took to him very well. My father, who was a pretty strict disciplinarian but a great man, saw a lot of potential in Alan. So they hit it off. Alan could talk everyone into anything.

I got on very well with Alan's father. His mother—that was another thing. Alan's mother worked; my mother never worked. We were different. I had never been in a family where the mother had gone to work. Work is part of everyone's life now; it was never part of mine. I found it terribly strange to go to their home and Mrs Bond was an accountant and would go out to work.

Mrs Bond was good to me. She taught me how to drive a car, how to cook. But as the years went along, we grew apart. I always called her 'Mrs Bond' until the day she died. It was a completely different family to mine. They were happy in their way, and we were happy in ours. Alan and I are both very strong people, and I guess Mrs Bond found me very strong too. We had a good relationship when the children were younger. I did not get on with her at all in her later years. Alan was very kind to his mother. I think Mrs Bond wanted more and more of Alan as she got older and she did anything to get his attention. I don't think I became a threat to her until her old age. We still spoke, but she became very demanding of Alan and he felt responsible for her.

She never asked me to call her by her Christian name, Kathleen. In part it was my mother's fault. She said, 'You've only got one mother, and that's me.' That was a very Irish way of looking at things. My daughters-in-law call me Eileen or Red. I was always respectful and called everybody 'Mrs'. I had friends who used to call their friends 'Aunty'. That was never heard of in our house. The lady who married my father for the second time was Mrs Law. I'd known her all my life and her daughter used to call my mother 'Aunty Mary', but I'd call her 'Mrs Law'. When Dad got married to her, in the late Seventies, he said to call her 'Thelma'. I found it so difficult. But that was me. It was just the way we were brought up.

Our lives were very much in the limelight, so that anything that Alan did was multiplied—beyond belief. You toss off rumours of other women for a long time, but eventually you have to stop and think about it. But Alan was no different to many men, I can tell you. What's the point in doing anything? There's a lot of girls willing to put their names to someone with power and money. A lot of stories go around. I never took them very seriously. We were still very happy even when these stories were abounding. I never thought anyone was a genuine threat to me. And still don't.

Unfortunately for Alan, his private life became very public. However, my private life at that time remained private. The papers weren't picking on me. They were just looking for anything negative Alan did, or anyone in a position like Alan's. I'm not Alan's keeper or judge, but there was certainly no-one who was ever a threat to Alan or our family. We are a very strong family. He loves his kids, still does. Even though Alan and I are divorced, our sense of family has not changed one bit. I'm very strong on that; we all are. Thank God for that.

Our children have all had a good education. This was important to both Alan and me. They had what was available to them and then they had to use it.

Our kids were at school in the morning and swimming in the afternoon. They had huge homework to do and sport. They all went to university except Susan, who pursued a riding career, but I look at Jody, who had many opportunities to say 'enough's enough' but she got through uni and then went back and did honours and then got accepted into Harvard. She really hasn't stopped all her life.

They seem to have the same drive that Alan has. It's different in the Eighties and Nineties to what it was in the Fifties. You have to do it all differently. A lot of men with entrepreneurial ability succeeded without a tremendous education and Alan always said that now you need the education to carry you through. The children hate publicity; they always have. Alan has always been in it, and generally accepted the good with the bad.

When the Sixties were moving ahead like crazy, I had my first overseas trip in '62. I loved it and never stopped after that. I made a tremendous amount of friends. I have always been one to be terribly busy.

I started looking at decorating. I had a huge opportunity to do all these things and I would find decorators' and designers' exhibitions all over the world, and started going to them. A lot of my friends are in that field. It's really about having an eye.

One of my best friends is a decorator and he comes in here and changes all the furniture around and as soon as he goes I put it all back again. We had completely different tastes in the Sixties. Sometimes I would go to North Fremantle and buy little houses for $8000 or $9000, and when the kids were at school I'd go to the house and I would do everything—not employ anybody. I renovated—up the ladder painting. One day my dad and brother had a business in Fremantle and I'd bought this house in North Fremantle. I was up the ladder and had painted the ceiling and  all the walls. I had paint everywhere and I went and borrowed my brother's ladder, which was varnished. When I brought it back he said, 'It's not my ladder. The one I lent you was varnished, and this one is white.' I had paint all over it. They all thought it was quite funny.

In the Seventies I did start doing a lot of decorating—a few very different jobs and a lot of run-of-the-mill. I did an aircraft for a Canadian company; spent a lot of time designing a seat belt with two colours. It looked fabulous—the whole effect was slightly Gucci. The belt wasn't approved as there wasn't enough strength in it to pass the safety regulations (a year later it was!). The company flew the plane over to show me—it was copied down to the last button! I spent weeks in Brisbane decorating the boat for the America's Cup—that is, the launch, not *Australia II*.

I'm not doing decorating now but am going to start consulting. A lot of people have asked me to come and help them. I have just done Craig's restaurant, Paparazzi. So that has been pretty constant. I was having lunch there recently with the designer/architect and he was saying it's time for a revamp. So we will have to give it a facelift. Restaurants have to be revamped constantly, otherwise people get sick of them.

But I could quite easily have a party every night and entertain. I love it. I never get sick of it. I enjoy people. I'm not mad about being on my own. I often have my parties at the restaurant.

Alan wasn't out every night. He was a very good father; still is. There were always loads of things going on, lots of lunches. In the Sixties my life was by the swimming pool with lots of girlfriends. They had to pick up their children so we started early. Not much drink when the kids were little. Maybe the Seventies were the time when we started drinking. Not that I've stopped in the Nineties. My health is quite good. I used to go to Sydney or Melbourne a lot and my favourite drink used to be champagne, but it's white wine now. My friends would pick up their children and bring them to the restaurant and I'd do the homework. We'd take them all home and go on to another party. Wild days. We'd talk about everything. Everybody's life was hectic. Always scandals and gossip going on.

A friend of mine is opening a salon at Georges and she wants me to come over. She's just rung me and she's been a very good friend and I love her dearly and she said, 'I'll die if you're not here.' I'll probably go. I don't go to Melbourne much now. But I go to Sydney because Jody's there.

In about '74 they started calling me 'Big Red'. As a child I was called Ginge and Blue and all those funny names they call redheads. It came with the America's Cup. They all used to call me 'Mrs Bond'. One of Susan's friends used to say to me, 'I can't call you "Mrs Bond" any more; I'll call you "Red".' But of course the Rhode Island Red is a chook. Nobody in Sydney calls me Red, but a lot in Perth call me Eileen as opposed to Red. It doesn't make much difference to me what they call me. I love Red; I don't care.

A lot of these boys and girls have been coming around here since they were little and now they're grown up. Craig was here yesterday with one of his friends having a beer and I was having a cup of coffee. And they sat down with me and watched Donahue and Oprah.

In '76 Alan was Australian of the Year. He had always had boats and had been doing boating races in the late Sixties and if he sailed to Bermuda I would fly and be there at the end, like a lot of yachting wives. I had been doing the racing circuit for a long time, being out on speedboats all day. I loved it. We always seemed to be on a boat somewhere on the Swan River. The kids all water-ski. Susan learned on the front of my skis.

When he told me about the America's Cup I thought he was totally mad. But he was always coming up with mad schemes. So off we went to Newport. I had already been in '72 when he had sailed in a Newport-to-Bermuda race, so I'd been there and knew the town pretty well. When we went there to sail in the Cup I got to know the people in Newport very well. So my life then took on another change. Newport is comprised of the people who live permanently in the town, yachting people and people who come in for the weekend to live in their mansions.

It was fairly rare to get to know the mansion people, but somehow or other I got to know them all immediately. So my life was filled with joy in Newport. I had the best of all worlds. Alan would be up trying to win this damned Cup and they'd have black-tie dinners every night up on the Hill and Alan would say 'I'm not going; I've got things to do.' So I went by myself. We were there for six months.

Snobs never had much effect on me. I just ignored them. The Newport people became very close friends, and still are. If I went to America I wouldn't dream of not ringing them. Eileen Slocum and Candy van Allan were two of my role models. Eileen's husband is a descendant from Joshua Slocum. They live in Rhode Island. I got to know Eileen because she was actually living in Newport and I went to many wonderful parties there with the President and Vice-President and generals. It was nothing to be sitting down next to General this or that. It wasn't that I was fascinated by their titles; I just say it as an aside of going to Newport. We would be sailing all day with the practices. I never got sick. Sailing, sailing all day then the long nights of black-tie dinners. I loved the conversation and meeting all those wonderful people. That world was so exciting. I would go to the parties and they'd say, 'Here comes Ei; here comes Red.' And they'd say, 'How is the boat going, darling?' They would come out with me sometimes for lunch, always, of course, to *the* beach club— Bailey's Beach, of which I am still a member.

But they weren't too pleased when we took the Cup away from them. Most of them don't live in Newport. They live in Washington and all over the place, but they did have a big interest in the New York Yacht Club. When it started to get serious in '83 at a couple of dinner parties they were a bit furious. They wanted me to discuss tactics, which I didn't consider I had much to do with, so I didn't.

Winning the Cup would have to be one of the highlights of my life. Ideally it would have been wonderful to be here when we won it, and especially great because that wonderful day the parade started in Fremantle, home of the South Fremantle Football Club. My dad played for Souths. He was president; also my brother held that position—and I am now the patron. The crew had been so rigidly trained they didn't know how to come off this training when they won. They couldn't just say, 'Well, let's relax and all get drunk together'. They were like machines; they walked sedately over to the house where we were having a buffet. It was really funny. We were all together, just the crew, with no-one going mad. It wasn't until we all got back here that we all just let go and thought, 'God, we made it!'

I knew Alan would get it one day. No-one had been so constant. And he was the only one who got up there to sail against them. Alan was certainly the sailing part of it, the crew and the sailing, but that never worried me because I'm not a sailor anyway. I felt I was there in my own right. Newport became very special to me. I go back all the time. Regardless of the America's Cup.

Going to Newport made me think differently. I realised the world was a much bigger place than Australia. I'd travelled to England a lot but in Newport I met the most exciting people. They were older than me and interesting. Their lives had just been so full. I really loved all that.

I was decorating madly, then. Anything we had—boats, apartments—but only for the business or friends.

I never felt I was being left behind. I mixed with the people that Alan mixed with. My life was and still is very full. We would have two business dinners a week during the Seventies and Eighties. I organised them all. Mostly sit-down dinners at home. We didn't entertain a lot in restaurants. Not like Sydney, where you always go out. Alan wouldn't have dreamed of asking people out for dinner; it always had to be here. It was always for twelve because there were twelve chairs. I couldn't do the cooking because they were mostly business people who hadn't met each other and the wives had come from another state with them, so it was imperative you were in there to introduce them and talk with them. That was good. I liked that.

I wouldn't be rude to anybody who came into the house. You don't have the choice of being rude if you are the hostess. But I have never had anyone in the house that I really couldn't stand, and we've had a lot of people through. I've got a good attitude to people; besides, you're not at the dinner table for that long. I'm very interested in people and when you are so busy with your life you don't think, 'Someone is trying to get to Alan through me.' You really don't. If people are disloyal you simply don't see them again. I have always known who my real mates are. Business is never easy; you don't get business and real friendship mixed up.

My life was very fulfilled. Alan was doing magic things, but I never thought, 'I'm not as good as you.' I didn't have anything to do with the business. I was involved in charity appeals. Channel 9 and I raised money, and every year I'd have a party. One year we got 100 in the lounge room listening to the opera with two people and a piano. It was an amazing night and everyone paid $1000. It's called the Pavilion Opera, a little English company who go around performing in big houses in England. They approached me and said they wanted to come to Australia and could I use them for anything. So I rang 100 people and asked if they would give $1000 for an appealathon, and they all said yes. The night was sublime, and we went outside under this wonderful canopy, and the stars were shining, and the caterers donated, and the florist donated. That was the Eighties.

I was on the board of the Fremantle Arts Centre from 1987 until 1991. Anything, in fact everything, to do with Fremantle has great interest for me. Visitors of mine always get to see Fremantle first, from the *Endeavour* project to the Fremantle Arts Centre.

Susanne's wedding was an extravaganza in the Eighties. In a way I'm sorry I did it, because every time Susanne comes up it's always the wedding. It never stops. And when Jody's wedding comes up, Susanne's does. We have had four weddings, all of them completely different. I just wish they would stop talking about Susanne's. Even Alan was surprised when he came home one night and said, 'There's a marquee in the river. Tell them to get it out; they're not allowed to put marquees up in the river.' And I said, 'It's for the wedding', and I thought he was going to have a heart attack. It was about three days before the wedding. In the speech he said it was fantastic.

Despite the rain I went to bed at six o'clock from Jody's wedding. The time just flew. People were there from four o'clock and by twelve o'clock they'd been there for eight hours. The first person said goodbye at two o'clock and I thought, 'What are they going for? It's really early!' and then I looked at my watch and nearly died. By the time we had the church, then the breakfast, then it poured and poured and we had umbrellas all the way out—and of course this was all adding to the fun. Jody was ecstatic, she was so happy, the rain couldn't have affected her less. And Alan said afterwards, 'Is this water on the floor?'

John Longley did the speeches. He was an amazing MC; he was just wonderful. He has been a yachting friend of ours forever. He used to sail a lot with Alan and now runs the *Endeavour* project.

I'm pretty old-fashioned. I like being supported and having doors opened. I'll probably get killed for saying that. Being liberated doesn't really mean having money. I really have always been liberated.

Alan's trial was the worst thing that ever happened. I've always got the best out of everything and the best side of this was knowing that our family could be so strong. I never knew there was such strength in all of us. It was just incredible. They were always there, all the time, but you don't have anything to show you that they're there until something dreadful happens. The strength of Alan was just amazing. I had never been in a courtroom in my life. But we've come through it.

I still go to church. My sense of faith was there during all that time, but I didn't actually sit in the court and pray. It was my worst nightmare.

A divorce is something you don't do overnight. You don't say the day before, 'I'm going to get a divorce.' Had I known what was going to happen, I don't know if I would have gone on with it. I don't think I would have piled that on top of Alan as well as everything else. It was just a matter between him and me. It was my decision. I wasn't terribly happy at the time, and it was a shock to everybody. Everybody thought we'd been together for so long, but then I never expected the year to be as bad as it was. Had I known all these terrible things were going to happen, divorce would have been the last thing on my mind. It was just between Alan and me, nothing to do with breaking up the family.

It was a very personal thing. Maybe Alan didn't listen, or I didn't listen to him. We weren't talking to each other very much. Communication had broken down.

I decided eighteen months before, and people say I did it to get Alan out of financial trouble and all that. Finance never came into it. They don't know me at all if they thought that. There was a big lack of communicating going on there for the past couple of years. Our lives had grown too far apart. I think you think that things will come all right because you've been through so much, but they didn't. I thought, 'Well, maybe it's time for me to do what my friends say I should do.' Having started the ball rolling, it's not easy to stop.

I thought it was time to get on with my own life. The children had all become independent and strong and capable. They understood my reasons and were happy about it. I looked back on my life and thought, 'What would I have done if my mother had divorced?' The thought that Susanne divorced rocked me. The family probably thought, 'Well, this one is home and hosed,' and then I go and do it after all those years. But you can't really be responsible for everything else. You've got to think of yourself.

After a divorce you suddenly seem to have a lot more time on your hands to do things. I would never sit and just be bored. The years of the divorce were a turmoil, but my life has never been anything but a turmoil. If it did any real harm to Alan I wouldn't have done it; that was my first consideration. I think we're both pretty strong people. We still see each other and we are talking to each other a lot more now. We were always great friends, and I think we've regained our friendship.

But divorce is not something I'd recommend to anybody. And being a Catholic comes into it, too.

I still feel I'm Mrs Bond. It just meant that maybe I could get on with my life and do other things. Yet he still is a prime consideration. What happened to Alan was grossly unfair and I didn't ever want to add to his struggles. But now I think we've come to enough conclusion to both be happy. He knew my loyalty would never waver. His would never waver to me. Until you get divorced you don't realise what people are saying about each other, and it's frightful. You think, 'She used to love this person!'

I was always committed to Alan. I didn't look at other

people. I would always stay with a commitment. I'm happy now if someone comes along I might think about. It's not happening at the moment.

If you've been married for a long time, it is nice being on your own. It's a new experience for both of us. I'm certainly not looking for anybody. I've been a married lady for a long time and now I'm not. I'm very happy with my life.

I was not very interested in politics. My father voted DLP—a long time ago. Dad was always on the Fremantle City Council, and I would often be walking the streets electioneering for him.

I am very positive. Always been so. I was born that way. I can always find something good about everything. Most problems are not insurmountable; you just have to get on with them. Life doesn't stop. Some of my friends say, 'This terrible thing happened,' and I say, 'Time's still ticking away.' Things change all the time in the world. You don't know what will happen tomorrow.

I love reading, I love listening to music. I read everything from Ken Follett to *French Lieutenant's Woman*. I've read everything that Bryce Courtenay has ever written. I have read all of John Grisham. I am now going back to Jack Higgins. *The Fatal Shore* was very hard to read, but it is worth the effort. Mary Wesley and Joanna Trollope I love to read on planes. *The Village Affair* was just terrific.

I just take life as it comes.

And then there has always been one of our children doing something. Jody was at Harvard last year and I used to go over and see her. Now she's in Sydney. Life's good. I've got more time now to think about what I really want to do. I like painting. I used to paint the walls. I set up a studio and did some marbleising just to see how it all works. I'm always painting pots in the garden. Gardening is becoming my big thing. I'll

get mad on something new and have to be good at it, and then I forget about it and think 'Well, I've done that now.' I took up spinning once. I sat there and spun until I nearly drove everybody insane. I had the spinning wheel and the long dress—the whole thing. Wool everywhere. My friends said to me, 'I can't believe it. When are you going to stop doing this?' I said, 'I've stopped now, because I can do it.'

This whole house is full of collected things. I'm always

collecting bits and pieces. I went through a stage where everybody gave me owls. I have got so many owls I can't tell you. Now they've stopped.

It's a very hard time in your life to commit yourself but I'm liking the degree of not committing myself. It's nice to drift. I may get involved with the Paraplegics Association and do some work for them.

I like living in Perth. I say hello to everybody and everybody says hello to me. I like that. It's very friendly.

I don't know what I've learned about life, really. I've often thought I would like to be a writer. I think it would be fascinating, but I can't write. I'm hopeless; I wouldn't know where to start. I just want to read and read, but who knows? One day you might read that Eileen Bond is the second Mary Wesley.

There have been endless times when I thought about taking up bridge or golf and then thought, 'No, not yet.'

I don't know what will happen in the next ten years. Maybe it will be a time for sitting back and reflecting. It's usually the case when you are coming up to the end of a century. I have always enjoyed what I'm doing. I think it's a shame if people don't enjoy their lives. We did try to keep our children right out of the public eye, but they have come to accept it. I don't really want the grandchildren to be in the media spotlight.

I'm dotty about my grandchildren, but they have a very wonderful mother and father who are the most devoted parents and strict. They keep a tight rein on them. We have one called Banjo after Banjo Paterson.

I think there will be more and more women coming to the top. The women are so strong in the States. Once when I was visiting Jody I went to a health farm in Canyon Ranch and it's fabulous. You sit at the table with all these women and the first thing they ask you is what you do and what business you are in. I have always found it very easy to say what I do, but this woman was really annoying me so I said nothing. And then she said, 'But what do you do? Aren't you in real estate? Well, what do you do?' And I said, 'Well, I'm loaded.' That shut her up. Another Australian woman came up too and we started laughing our heads off. 'Loaded' can mean something else in America. They are so inquisitive into what you do with your life. These are high-powered women who have taken two days off work to get there and get home. The husbands are all looking after the children.

I think the relationship between men and women is changing dramatically. But the fact that Alan worked and I stayed home never upset me. I would never want to be where Alan was.

Who knows what would have happened to us both if we hadn't married each other? In my day you made a commitment and you stayed there. But you have to have a stamina and belief in that person. I never felt downtrodden. I would drop the kids off to school and then go and do my own thing. You have to find something you're not tied to. I didn't have to be there the next day. I could take forever to do it. My son and daughter-in-law work together so well. He does equally as much with the children. It's a new era and it's exciting. I always look forward to tomorrow.

When I finally turned off the tape recorder, Eileen said, 'Where are you staying? I'll give you a lift.' She invited me to have a look around while I waited for her to get ready. I strolled into the main living-room with its balcony overlooking the river. It was large but not ostentatiously so. The furnishings were by top-class designers, but not glitzy, and the mantelpiece was full of silver-framed photos of Alan or Eileen with famous people such as the Pope, the Royal Family, prime ministers and so on. It felt like a large family home, not a place where business people had been entertained.

Later that day, Eileen phoned me at my hotel and suggested that she take me to breakfast the next morning. Her tone was friendly and hospitable. We met at an outdoor restaurant right on the beach at Fremantle. After we had eaten she offered to take me for a drive around Fremantle. As we walked to her car, various people smiled and said hello to her. She smiled back. 'I like living here,' she said. 'It's still a friendly country town, really.' Certainly I had encountered no hostility when I mentioned her name; nor had I seen it on the faces of the people in the restaurant.

As we drove around Fremantle she chatted, pointing out places of interest. I asked her about how she coped when Alan went to prison. Her face clouded over. 'Well, it's not something you can prepare yourself for—it was a terrible shock. It's not anything that I ever imagined would happen. But we banded together as a family and worked hard to get the evidence that we knew would get him out. Alan never speaks of it. Neither do I. When things like that happen you deal with them at the time and then after they're over you get on with your life. There's no point in dwelling on them or getting bitter and twisted about it. We never speak of it as a family. There's no point in the grandchildren hearing about it all the time.' The subject was closed.

I moved on to the famous people she has met. 'The Pope was my favourite. Did you see that photo at home of me speaking to him, and Alan's in the background with an expression on his face that shows he was thinking, "Now what's she saying to him?" In fact I had said to the Monsignor who was looking after the tour, "Tell him he must have blessed the wrong bloody boat." So the Monsignor went and told the Pope. And the Pope replied to me in Italian that he was highly amused by my remark. Alan never quite knows what I'm likely to say ...

'Then there was President Ronald Reagan. Regardless of his

politics, he had a nice warmth to him. She was different, a bit of a dolly-bird type. I haven't read Kitty Kelley's book; I thought she was a bit unreliable in some of her sources.

'Princess Di was nice, but not nearly as good-looking in the flesh. She's attractive, but clearly the camera is magic for her. Some people are like that, aren't they?

'Then there was the time when Fergie and Joan Collins turned up at a do in the same Yves St Laurent dress. Fergie looked pretty amused, but not Joan.'

On the way to the airport I asked the taxi driver about the Bonds. He launched into a diatribe about Alan.

'But what about Eileen?' I asked.

'Red? Oh, she's a happy-go-lucky sort. Stuck by him, that's for sure.'

Betty Churcher

A couple of years ago it seemed as if every paper or magazine I picked up had a story on Betty Churcher, the first woman to be a director of the National Gallery. She seemed to have suddenly come out of nowhere into the glare of the media's headlights. Everything I read made me more curious to find out about her life.

When I did meet her for the first time, I was very impressed not only with her style, her charm and her famous open smile, but more importantly with the strong sense of herself that was almost tangible.

She is different from many of the women in this book because for those outside the art world Roy Churcher, her partner, is not necessarily a very well-known name. For many years of their life together, however, it was Roy whose name was the only one in the spotlight.

Betty is what is now termed 'a late bloomer'. If the saying 'early ripe, early rotten' is true, there's definitely something to be said for delaying fruition.

She picked me up from the airport and drove me to the house, thirty minutes out of Canberra, which she and Roy had designed especially for their needs. As we entered, Roy emerged from the kitchen to greet us, saying, 'One of our sons just said, "Oh no, Dad, you're not going to be in the kitchen when she arrives! It's such a reverse stereotype!"' I was delighted that he was, because the sauce he made for our lunchtime pasta was delicious!

Betty and I spent the entire day sitting at the table on the wooden verandah overlooking their ten hectares on the banks of the Yass River, complete with a Fred Williams hill. Various of Betty and Roy's four sons, who were staying with them over Christmas, popped out to say hello and get their mother's advice on various things.

Betty has that special skill of making whoever she is talking to the centre of her attention.

WHEN I was ten or eleven I desperately wanted to be a boy. It dawned on me that being a girl was going to be a problem. Mum and Gran were very focused on my brother Ian and I felt terribly badly done by. Whether I was or not, I really don't know. I used to dream about being unfairly treated and wake up in the morning with the dream still with me. These dreams went on for quite a few years. I had a feeling of deep frustration because I could see ahead that as a woman I had a ball and chain around my leg.

I was christened Elizabeth but I was always called Betty. I don't know whether I have to blame Betty Hutton or the Queen, who was called Betty when she was a little girl. Knowing Mum, it was probably the Queen, who's about four years older than me.

My earliest memory is when I was something like two, on a rocking chair with my brother Ian on one arm of the chair and my cousin Jim on the other. They were rocking with some vigour and my mother raced out and reprimanded them and snatched me up off this chair. Obviously they were about to buck me off and this was the game. I was not in the least bit scared. I can remember loving it, and wondering why I was being snatched up. I also have an early memory of the entire dining room. I was in a high chair still and Ian was sitting at the table, and I couldn't understand why I couldn't sit at the table.

I was born in January 1931 and in that time and in some people's minds it is still all about the male child. In Mum and

Gran's minds the female child was more or less an insurance policy for your old age—someone who would look after you. My Gran lived between her two daughters, my mum and my aunt. Gran had been a rather grand lady and had never had to do anything, as she had servants right up until after the war.

Gran would come around to the house with a bag of sweets and give them all to Ian. This was acceptable behaviour. Mum's explanation in later years was that Ian had been so sick as a child and that Gran had looked after him. But it was all about being the one who was going to carry on the family name. I did resent him for that, which was rather sad because we now have a very nice relationship, but it took a long while. Dad, on the other hand, was over-rigorous with Ian in terms of bringing him up as a man. I was very much Daddy's girl, but he was a travelling salesman and so he was not there a lot. I always felt that I had lost my protector and ally.

After I'd had three children I said to Mum, 'How could you have singled out one child like that?' She'd give him a shilling pocket money and she'd give me sixpence. When there's eighteen months between you, the oldest doesn't need twice as much lemonade or ice-cream. She just said, 'Well, darling, he's a boy.' There was no malice in her voice.

When I was growing up the wireless was where the TV now stands. Dad had his chair, which was sacrosanct, and then there was a sofa on which Ian often lay full length. One day I suddenly heard this piece of music on the wireless that I wanted to hear, so I raced in from wherever I was and just perched on the arm of the sofa. Dad did his block because Ian had stayed lying stretched out on the sofa and hadn't made room for me. I didn't want room on the sofa because I was only perching to hear this bit of music, but my grandmother the next day in the laundry really tore strips off me: 'Selfish little girl. You put your brother through that terrible ordeal with your father losing his temper.' I was constantly finding myself caught in these sorts of situations.

Gran had migrated out here in about the 1850s by sailing ship. She tells of leaving London just as she was about to be a debutante, and when I went over to London to study, I discovered a house exactly like hers in South Kensington, just like 'Upstairs, Downstairs'. When she came to Brisbane, Queen Street was a dirt road; Creek Street was in fact a creek with a little bit of water. She said she cried for about a week. For her father it was all a grand adventure and she was one of eight. She married a man who was very wealthy with cattle properties, so Mum grew up in those circumstances, but she married a Scot from a very different background. When I went over to England for the first time in 1952 I visited two old aunts who lived at Broadstairs. It was one of those rare sunny days and I had to go and sit in this crusty old house and listen to them going through the family history. They said, 'And Veda Huffen, she married rather unsuitably, I believe, didn't she? Some rather disreputable Scot, I seem to remember.' 'Yes,' I said. 'That was my father.' Totally put them off. They went on about family heirlooms and in desperation I said, 'Look, Aunt Cecily, I really don't put a great deal of stress on all this.' She sat forward in her chair and said, 'But my dear, you should! You would if you were buying a horse,' which has become one of our family jokes. We always say, 'You would if you were buying a horse.'

I think I am very like my father. He was very internalised— a man of great potential who never realised it, mainly because of his beginnings. He ended up as a salesman in the Vacuum Oil Company, totally frustrated. His father was a Presbyterian minister in Edinburgh and his mother died when he was three. The father then remarried and the new wife would have nothing to do with my father and his sister. They were farmed out—he went to his grandmother, and I think he always felt very bitter about that. He had very little schooling, right up at Loch Tay in northern Scotland with an old grandmother who spoke Gaelic and very little English. He had few options. I adored him; he was a marvellous man.

I don't know really how my mother came to meet him. It was a funny relationship. Mum was thirty-two when she married. At that time thirty-two was well and truly on the shelf. I heard later that my grandmother, the one who wept for a week when she came out to Australia, was a very wild young thing. An aunt told me that she used to shock the Brisbane establishment by riding up Queen Street with a five-in-hand, which women never ever did. She used to flirt shamelessly with all of her daughters' beaux, so my aunt and my mother both married very late—she probably frightened them all away.

My mother just did everything for my father. Once when Mum was sick I had to go over because Dad literally couldn't make a cup of tea. I said, 'Mum, I don't believe this!' She said, 'No, dear, he can't, he really can't.' I said, 'Boiling water and pouring it?' 'No,' she said. 'He doesn't know about these things.' It was true. All through my early life Gran paid for servants and I was never allowed in the kitchen at all, at any stage. That's why I never, naturally, learned how to cook.

It was a house that my grandfather, who was a Queensland government architect, designed for his daughter. I didn't much like it, but it was very much to my father's taste—lots of wood-panelled walls, which I thought very gloomy, but he loved it because it reminded him of Scotland. I remember a maid teaching me to do handsprings and I bet she wouldn't have been more than sixteen. They lived in, poor little things.

All that stopped with the Second World War, but Mum had never handled a child. When I had children and I'd be doing someone's nappy and one of the others was crying I'd ask

Mum to pick the baby up for two minutes. 'Oh no, dear,' she'd say, 'I don't think I could do that.' She'd always had a nursery maid. I'd say, 'Mum, I'm frantic!' because all my children came in fairly quick succession.

She'd say, 'Oh dear, I know.' All her stories were about the terrible time Ian burned his hand and the maid had just put the afternoon tea-tray down. I'd say, 'Give me a break!'

I hated public school when I started. Then Gran sent me to Somerville House and Ian was at Church of England Grammar School. The headmistress, Miss Craig, engendered in you this sense of responsibility and the importance of each girl's individuality. She was an extraordinary woman, and she did wonderful things for me. Unfortunately she died before I got back from England, so I couldn't thank her.

I was clever, but I don't think I ever applied myself seriously to study. Very early on it became apparent I had this one thing that I did well, and that was to draw. Art was what it was about, and I could see that this was how I was going to climb the ladder. So that's all I cared about. It pleased Dad a great deal that I could draw, but Mum was determined that I should do a secretarial course. Dad saved me from that. I got so upset that he said to Mum, 'Don't ever mention it again.'

I could draw anything. It's like a person with perfect pitch. I didn't realise that it wasn't possible for everyone to draw what they saw. I thought the only thing I could do was to commercialise, although I had no idea what that meant. All I was focused on was art. Miss Craig rang Dad up and said that if he would allow me to continue at school without fees—it was an expensive school—I could teach in the Junior School. So I was student teacher for the last two years at high school. That was a fantastic thing for her to do, because I would never have got into the Royal College if I hadn't had matriculation. I loved the teaching.

I was tall, I was lean, I was lanky and everything that one shouldn't be. When I got to adolescence in the Forties women were meant to be bosomy, little waists, big bottoms. I had none of them. It did worry me. No-one would ever ask me to dance at school dances. I would go and sit on the side and loathe it. It was horrible. Once when Dad was driving me to the Milton Tennis Club with my bony shoulders sticking out of a strapless taffeta dress with nothing to hold it up, I remember thinking, 'I'd rather be doing anything in the jungles of Africa than what I am about to have to do.' I had a sudden revelation: *you don't have to do it!* I was fifteen and I never went to another dance. I wouldn't go to dances or to tennis parties, even though Mum urged and urged. I would stay at home and read, or draw and paint.

I was vice-captain and captain of the house and I had lots of friends that I still retain from those days who were interested in art. Anne Thompson was one who has continued to paint. I was not interested in boys, nor were they interested in me. The idea of marriage just wasn't there. I was very involved in trying to become an artist. Miss Craig was not concerned about my being an artist but she was concerned about everybody excelling in some way. Being a good wife and mother would have been part of that, too, but you'd have to do it with some intelligence. She was pretty extraordinary. Pat Prentice, my art teacher, who is now living in Brisbane and still painting, was an absolute role model for me when I was an assistant teacher.

When I left school I had to immediately start earning and contributing towards the household. I had to pay board, so I immediately took a teaching job in my old school, which served, but I remember being very upset about not going to art school. My dad did not think it was important and my mum thought it was unnecessary. He thought that education would spoil me and give me ambitions and ideas about myself which would make me a difficult wife. Mum hoped that I would meet Mr Right and all would be well. My brother went to the university, studied engineering and has done very well. I became bored. I thought, 'I have to get out of Brisbane. This isn't going to work. I am not going to be a teacher for the rest of my life in a girls school.' I really wanted to be a painter.

A lot of my life has been ostensibly good luck. When Jill Ker Conway came back to Australia she said that it was amazing how often women who have become successful through hard work say it was luck, and I thought to myself, 'How often have I said I have been very lucky?' Anyhow, I was the president of the Young Artists' Group, which was part of the Royal Queensland Art Society. I was contacted by a junior reporter of the *Courier-Mail* who obviously wanted to promote his career, who said, 'Why don't you initiate a travelling scholarship for the Young Artists' Group?' He said that the Art Society could supplement what we raised dollar for dollar. I thought it was fantastic and that this might be my escape hatch. To my horror, the next day on the leader page the new scholarship was announced, with the Royal Queensland Society subsidising it dollar for dollar. I got a message to see the president of the Society. They were boxed into it. The Young Artists' Group of the Royal Queensland Society had annual exhibitions and I had been selling pictures for five guineas and six guineas. We organised pavement exhibitions never before seen in Brisbane. All of the proceeds went into the scholarship. We raised 300 guineas. For the competition we had to produce a figure composition, a still life and a figure drawing. I don't know what I would have done if I hadn't won. My fallback position was Melbourne, but there was no money.

There were three judges, and when I was called to the phone and told that I had won the scholarship I had never known such a feeling of elation. On the train home I kept thinking, 'I'll be seeing Paris! I will be in London! I am out of it!' I can't describe what it felt like. The nearest thing I could have imagined would have been solitary confinement for fifteen years in gaol in the dark and suddenly the door opens and you are out. I knew that the real world was elsewhere. I knew that it wasn't going to happen for me in Brisbane, which was extraordinarily contained. Of course, it is totally different now. Mum wasn't too sure about me taking off, but it was just sheer bliss to be on my own. I had the most extraordinary sense of freedom.

I didn't share a cabin with anyone and I had my first shipboard romance. I was totally unworldly. I look back with horror at the time in Colombo where the boat had stopped and an Indian sidled up to me and said, 'Come and see a very special temple.' I went off with him and when I realised I couldn't see another white person I really thought I'd had it. On one occasion he nearly pulled me into a male toilet. I resisted quite violently and he desisted. I think he had been sent off by a jewellery shop to pick up people and take them to the shop where they could spend money. He had other plans. I kept talking about my husband on board ship. I was really scared that I would never get back there. At one stage he bought me a coconut, broke it and poured the milk into a glass, which was the filthiest glass that I have ever seen. I thought, 'What is the best? Is it better to die by being strangled or to die of some terrible type of cholera or typhoid?' I didn't and it was perfectly all right. I was never more relieved than when he brought me back to the ship.

My romance with a member of the crew resulted in my thinking I was pregnant. I thought, 'I'll go up to Coventry, out of London and have this baby there and no-one will ever know about it.' I had no idea about abortion or what to do. I thought the only option was to have it secretly. Why I thought of Coventry, I'll never know. It must have happened to a lot of Australian girls. With great relief I discovered I wasn't pregnant. I was supposed to be staying with an aged aunt who was living in London in Earl's Court. By the time I met her she had cancer and was almost off the planet. She was an archaeologist and one of the first women to receive an honorary doctorate from Oxford. She was an Egyptologist and had a lot of interesting artefacts in the place, but she was absolutely paranoid about men. Convinced that men were going to invade her territory, she had nailed all the windows of her flat down. She told me that the one condition of my staying with her was that no male would ever enter the house. She died very soon after that and then two more oldish, retired women who had owned a bookshop moved in downstairs and they had similar views. They were kind old sticks, but they were not going to have men after hours or any of that nonsense. I remember one boyfriend and I had rehearsed walking downstairs to the front door so they would hear two pairs of feet. We'd say quite loud goodbyes and the door would close. I would then walk back so there was just a single pair of feet, and he was to tiptoe without the shoes. Just as he was tiptoeing past with the shoes in his hand they opened the living room door and caught him. We had to make some extraordinary excuse and he had to go.

In London I had a lot of help from Robert Haines, who was then the director of the Queensland Art Gallery—he became the director of the David Jones Gallery in Sydney for many years, and is now in France. He had given me a whole address book of addresses. I was about to go to the Byamshaw Art School. Robert said, 'Don't go there. I've got a friend who is the head of a school at Southwest Essex Technical College called Walthamstowe—go there.' If I had gone to Byamshaw, God knows what would have been the result.

Walthamstowe was a feeder school for the Royal College of Art. I studied there for about eighteen months as a preparation for the Royal College. I was living on the scholarship and the flat was very cheap—about one pound fifty a week. I worked very hard for the entrance exam. They had about three hundred applicants of whom they selected twenty-five. You had to submit a folio of drawings and three or four paintings. They selected about one hundred and then cut that down to twenty-five through a process of an examination and an interview. It was a totally male staff and the interview was like an audience with the Pope. What they were testing was your commitment, and of course there was no doubt about that in my case. My commitment was very clear and rock solid. I could not conceive of there being anything else in life and I believed in my talent unquestionably at that time because I had done nothing but well.

When I went to the Royal College in 1954 I felt absolutely fabulous. In retrospect I think it was probably pretty awful. The staff just left you alone, more or less. The only thing that I can remember from the Royal College that was of real use, although at the time I didn't think it was, was what old Ruskin Spear said. I used to go drinking with him at the pub in Hammersmith, but he had never said anything to me about my work. I'd just won a prize; they used to have a summer competition where they'd give you a subject and over the long summer break you had to do a big picture composition. On this occasion it was 'I opened the door and only one looked up'. I'd gone out and got these two old guys sitting on a park bench and asked them if they would pose for me for five shillings a session. I painted a picture which was influenced by Cézanne's *Card Players*, but these old guys in my painting were playing dominoes. I won the competition in my first year, so I was feeling pretty pleased and proud of myself. I was walking along with Ruskin Spear and wondering would he say anything complimentary. I was just longing for praise. And he said, 'You know what's the trouble with you?' And I remember thinking, 'Oh, what's he going to say now?' And he said, 'You try too hard.' And I thought to myself, 'You silly old chump. How can you try too hard?'

Looking back I know now what he meant. I didn't allow any of my intuitive and instinctive forces to enter. I would have an image so clear in my head of what I wanted to make that I didn't allow any serendipitous accidents to carry me off into flights of fancy. I was rigidly screwing it down. That comes out of a certain confidence and relaxation, which I probably didn't have. But also I wonder whether that imaginative thing was really there. I don't think I was an imaginative painter. I think I was a good painter and an intelligent painter. Now I think he was probably right. In a lot of my life I try too hard— I try to force things into a mould which I have preconceived instead of rolling with the punches.

Recently the prime minister had drinks for the public servants and gave a talk which was so good. I was in the middle of industrial strife, which was to my mind terribly frustrating because I had the 'Dressed to Kill' exhibition, which was obviously going to be a great success. I had all of this thumping away at the back of my head and he said, 'Don't forget the big vision, the big picture.' He was saying don't worry about your carriages rocking from time to time, as long as you just keep

going. I think I try to keep my carriages too straight and get frantic if they start to rock and people are trying to derail you. Of course they will try and derail you all along the line. Right through my life I really have tried to map a course and then follow it—probably too rigidly.

I met Roy Churcher by accident. I was invited to someone's bedsitter who was at the Slade School of Art. I was living almost completely on white bread and jam and there were all these goodies in the kitchen. I was jolly hungry and I was eating one meat mince pie after another. Roy evidently said, 'Don't bring that girl back to this flat ever again.' So that was the first meeting and it wasn't kapow! I had my eyes on someone else who was also at the Slade at the time. But Roy came along to a college party and it just went from there. We got married in 1955, so it was fairly quick. We were at Poole Harbour and I'd got into a rowboat we had hired and he was about to step in and I said, 'How about getting married?' and poor Roy nearly upset the boat. The reason our relationship has survived all sorts of vicissitudes is that we have always been terrific comrades. We are very best mates and that is why I could propose to him. There was none of that knight-on-a-white-charger stuff. I'd had that with previous people and it probably would have been a disastrous marriage based on a passionate sort of obsession. I didn't have that with Roy, but he was the person I wanted to be with. He was the most interesting to talk to, and that's been with us all our lives. We don't have boring moments. If one of those ones I was obsessional about had swept me off my feet I probably would have married them, but they just didn't ask. Miss Coleson and Miss Wiltshire who lived below still kept a watchful eye out for men, and it was very frustrating. We thought, why make it hard for ourselves? So Roy said okay. I think he had thought we would eventually live together, but I don't think he had thought of marriage as such. At that time divorce was not an impossible thought. I can remember thinking, 'Well, if it doesn't work out we could always get out of it.' It was a funny wedding, because I can't dressmake at all but I made my own dress. I must have looked like nothing on earth. It was a registry office wedding with just our friends. I remember Peter Freeman standing at the back rolling a cigarette and the celebrant saying, 'Excuse me, this may not be a church but please wait for your cigarette until later.' We had a little reception, but mostly it was about making it possible to have something of a love life. The flat had now become really cheap because the rent didn't alter but students were not supposed to get married and retain their grants so we had to do this in great secrecy. My parents knew and Dad wrote one of those Victorian fathers' letters about how Roy was now captain of the ship. It was so Victorian and Scottish, all about taking over the helm. Roy was so amazed by this notion he couldn't ever answer it because he just didn't know what to say.

We began our relationship as equal partners because Roy was so appalled at the thought of being the captain of the ship. It really offended Dad that he never answered, but he just didn't know how to explain that we had quite a different relationship. It was quite advanced for a man in 1955, although I'm not sure that he didn't think that his career was going to be more important than mine, but he would never have voiced it. By being married I could have a love life, have a best friend and I could get on with being an artist. That's how it was right up until I decided to have children.

I decided that Roy should meet the family because I had stayed away for five and a half years and I thought this was a bit rough. I was fully intending to return to Britain. I left a whole furnished flat. Roy's brother moved in to house-sit while we were away. At one stage Roy said if we stayed two years he could emigrate and get out for five pounds. But we paid ninety pounds each, which was the fare. I wasn't even prepared to stay for the two years. I was very career orientated. I thought I had to make my career in London; it was no good doing it in Brisbane. Roy's background is working class. His mother was an orphan and he doesn't know much of her background. If you look at his green eyes I'm sure quite a lot of him is Irish. His father was a night-shift worker at a cable factory. He was the one that first got reasonable working conditions for workers and Roy was a member of the Socialist Party of Great Britain. I was mystified by Roy being so fiercely political.

It didn't occur to me to think about who was the most talented. When I finished at the Royal College I carried off nearly all of the prizes. I won a travelling scholarship, I won the drawing prize over the whole of the college, which was very prestigious, and I got a first-class pass, which only about two or three achieved. Roy didn't do as well, so I was really at that stage a much more successful practitioner than he was. I never felt competitive. I don't know whether he did or not. It wasn't an issue between us at that stage. It became a bit of an issue when we came back to Australia and people called him Roy Cameron and I don't think he liked that. I thought I'd stay Betty Cameron professionally, but it somehow became a bit inoperable. Even now when I've got to sign a whole lot of things, suddenly out of all these 'B. Churchers' a 'B. Cameron' will appear, which is amazing after all these years.

So we came back to Australia in 1957 and lived with my parents for a little while. They then went overseas because Dad had retired, so we had the house to ourselves. While they were away we decided we would do them a service and brighten up their house. This was when the latest thing was Tibetan Gold, and the bedroom was lavender all over. We thought it was marvellous and so modern. In retrospect it was hideous! Dad must have nearly died when he saw his oak panelling with paint on it. The Fifties were terrible. But we thought we were very smart.

At first I did exam marking. Then I did some part-time teaching at the Brisbane Tech because the painting instructor was away. Travelling on a tram back to Holland Park where

Mum and Dad lived, I was sitting next to a commercial artist and telling him of our dilemma when he said that the old School of Art in Brisbane had an attic just under the roof which was empty, and why didn't I see if I could rent that and start up an art school? The Brisbane Tech was still, to my horror, exactly as I had left it. Nothing had changed since 1912. They had to draw from the antique cast and you didn't paint in colour for the first two years. It was all to do with old academic training which, now that I'm sixty-three, I think is probably not a bad thing. At least they learned how to paint. Art schools now are all about ideas, and I believe ideas are either there or they're not, but to put your ideas into any sort of shape you need a few techniques.

This attic was like an oven in the summer; it was filthy, and we had no taps in the studio. We had to scrub the floor, and you'd scrub an area the size of a table and the water would be black with mud. So you'd have to carry it down two flights of stairs, empty it out, fill it up, bring it back and scrub another small area. I've never known anything like the Brisbane heat under this tin roof.

We started classes there and it was just the right time, because people so wanted something. There had been a lot of 'local girl makes good' publicity when I came home. It was a private art school and we had day and evening classes. I hung wet rags in front of an electric fan to try and make it possible for the students because they just couldn't put up with the summer heat.

We taught there together for about a year and then Jon Molvig, whom I later wrote a book about, decided to leave Brisbane. I went over to Molvig's studio and asked if he would let us take it over. He did, but it was a bit touchy, because he had been very antagonistic toward Roy because he hated Englishmen. He was very macho and very aggressive and if you were prepared to drink with him into a stupor and end up in a fight you were mates for life. Roy was not that sort of man, so he was never accepted. Molvig gave him hell. By this time we had purchased a house at Kangaroo Point near the studio with some money my grandfather had left me. It was a tiny fibro house. I think it cost 3000 pounds. That's when I started a family.

I was pregnant when I was painting the Queensland Centenary Art Prize, and Ben was born in August of 1959. I had always wanted children. Mum would never let me bring friends home unless I warned her in advance in case the house was not looking just so. She always used to bathe at four p.m. and get dressed with her corsets and the full bit no matter what the weather, in readiness for Dad coming home from work. I really wanted to provide the absolute alternative environment—free and easy. They could come and go, their friends could come and go—quite different. Unfortunately, we always go to extremes and I think I probably made it too free and easy.

Roy was not much of a cook at that stage. I was doing more, but with my nose glued to the recipe book. There was not an awful lot of housework being done by either of us because when we were teaching at Kangaroo Point we had no car. We didn't even have a bank account. We used to take in money from the students and put it in a tin. We didn't have money for furniture—we had orange boxes with a little bit of material across the front on an extender wire as bedside tables. The wardrobe was a shelf with a curtain around it on big rings. We had no money at all and yet in a funny way we have never seemed to have more money. It was always our money together, never, 'This is yours and this is mine.' We were happy, except that I really wanted to go back to England. I did not and never have liked Brisbane. Roy loved it. It was everything

Roy had dreamt of as a child in wartime London. Suddenly here was this beautiful tropical paradise and he very quickly got in with Ray Hughes, who became his dealer and launched Roy's career. I had one exhibition when we first arrived, at Johnson's Gallery, of drawings, which didn't do terribly well because they weren't saleable things. But I never exhibited in Brisbane.

When I discovered I was pregnant, which wasn't planned, I was thrilled. But returning to London would have been too hard. Roy was blossoming in his career and having a wonderful time. His was not a monogamous nature. I was terribly jealous and terribly threatened and felt so helpless. With young children and no money, what could you possibly do and if you left how could you possibly manage? I wanted four children. I kept going even though it totally wrecked my confidence. It was all very Sixties and free love. I was battling the times, because there was a lot of it going on. We eventually worked through it. I don't want to go on about it now.

I stopped painting when I had the first child, and that was a decision that I made, partly because I was terrified of being an indifferent painter or an indifferent mother. I really wanted to do the family thing well. I wanted to give my children the kind of life that I didn't believe I'd had as a child. Roy's career was steaming ahead and Brisbane in the Sixties was not very conducive for women's careers or for women. It was very 'redneck' country, much more so than the rest of Australia.

I liked being a mother and still do. The children are the single most important thing in my life. They were then and they are now. I thought that I might pick up being an artist again after the children, but there have been no regrets. I don't actually think it's the result of not having time and being suddenly engulfed in children. I really do think that I had reached the next hump in my career. I had been very successful; I'd surged ahead. Then I had to push over the next big hill, to move from being a very bright art student to being a good artist and then, you hope, a brilliant artist. I'm not all that certain now that I have that intuitive imagination to do it. I think probably if I had been a single woman, if I had no children and that was my only way to go, I might have got through that period where I was floundering. I was like a swimmer trying to get to the end of the pool and the end of the pool was never coming. But I had an alternative and to some people, some artists, there really is no alternative. That remark of Ruskin Spear's which keeps echoing in my head, 'The trouble with you is you try too hard' ...

I wasn't jealous of Roy having a terrific career, not in the least, because it was my decision. When I had two children I thought I would start painting again. We were still living in Kangaroo Point and I had a verandah. The children were having their afternoon sleep so I closed the doors onto the verandah and set up my easel. They both woke up and got out of bed. Two little kids with their nappies on were clawing at the glass doors. I ignored them at first and got on with it and then I thought, 'This is ridiculous. You've got to have a studio, you've got to have a nanny, you've got to have all of those things if you are going to really do it.' And I didn't have the means. But there's not an ounce of me that regrets that and I have a very strong suspicion, but it can only be that, that I probably wouldn't have made it anyway. I'm a very obsessional person and I think that obsession to succeed got transferred. I became an obsessional mum and still am. They are now much older than I was when I was having babies and I'm still watching over them. It drives Roy bonkers, but I'd sell up everything if they needed the money. My top priority is their well-being and happiness. With everything I do there is an obsessional edge. I have to push it to its limits. Being a mother will last to the end of my life—it's not something I can turn off. My financial advisers keep beseeching me to stop. They tell me to put the money aside because the children are living off my retirement package, but that doesn't matter to me. Roy

is still a full-time artist and we both pay the bills. Money doesn't worry me—I'd be quite happy to live simply at the end of my life.

I had decided that I would not return to full-time work until the youngest went to school. Roy had been teaching full-time at the Brisbane Tech and loathing it and really wanting to get into the studio. When Tim started school I resigned from a lot of part-time jobs and accepted a full-time job at the Kelvin Grove Teachers' College.

Roy was terrific as a dad—marvellous.

Moving into Kelvin Grove was really the beginning of my

professional career. The Sixties was my bad decade. It made me loathe Brisbane and that has never stopped. I was unhappy and insecure and Brisbane was applauding it. The Seventies were good because I worked for eight years at Kelvin Grove and I had someone to look after the kids. We moved from Kangaroo Point to Indooroopilly to a much bigger house where we could have a live-in housekeeper. Roy had started to do the cooking. I was not overly worried about the housework, but I don't like chaos. I'm not Mrs Housewife, and certainly the thing that I like least about housekeeping is cooking. I don't mind washing or ironing because it is visible, whereas cooking is, like, it's down, it's gone and you've just got to wash the damn dishes. I don't place a great deal of importance on food and I think that to be a good cook you've got to be something of a gourmet yourself. My son Peter is a gourmet cook and if he were travelling overseas half of it would be to see the art galleries of the world and the other half would be to eat in the best restaurants. For me it would be just to see the art galleries. Art feeds me in a way that nothing else can. I can stand in a gallery looking with great intensity and doing drawings all day and I feel no physical strain. I feel nothing until I walk out and then my knees nearly buckle underneath me. It's my private passion and is now my public passion because of my job. I really don't know why it should be like this. Perhaps it was because as a small girl it was the one thing I seemed to be able to do better than anyone else, particularly my brother, and I got praise for it. Whatever it is, it was there from the very beginning.

I loved teaching art history. I loved trying to make people realise just what was so special about Monet. I'm a very good lecturer, I don't have to be coy about it. I was teaching practical art as well, which started to become a worry for me because I'd stopped practising and then I realised I had worked

myself into a funny situation because I was very highly qualified as a practising artist—I had a first-class diploma from the
Royal College of Art and I had won all of those awards—but
in art theory and history I had no academic qualification at all.
That's when I decided that I really wanted to stop teaching
practice and go on to art history and furthermore to become
qualified. In 1976 I went to the Courtauld Institute, which is
the Fine Art Institute of London University and without a
doubt the place to go. I had study leave from Kelvin Grove
and we all went on the money I got from my first book, *Understanding Art*, which I'd written at Kelvin Grove specifically
for students in art school. I was a bit worried about my MA at
Courtauld because I had never done a BA. You had to do two
exams and a thesis and, as is my nature, I would have to do
well. I gave it my best and did very well.

When I came back I taught the one year required at Kelvin
Grove and Brian Siedel invited me to apply for a lecturing job
in Melbourne, which worried me. I thought perhaps I might
not measure up. I left Roy in Brisbane with the four boys
while I went off to test the temperature and found that I really
enjoyed teaching much better there.

I went home a couple of times during that year—lots of
phone calls, but nevertheless it was not a huge amount of contact. It was a long break and I was living in students' halls of
residence, which was a bit of a nightmare. I was writing a
book for Rigby's for schools about Australian painting post-
Second World War. All the history books only take you up to
the Second World War. When I bought the house in Melbourne, which I found in relation to the school I wanted the
kids to go to, I had one carton of rough stuff and all of the fair
copy in another carton. I said, 'Now, this pile goes to the dump
and this pile goes to the new house in Brunswick,' and they
took the fair copy to the dump. I had worked for twelve

months on that text and it was gone. I felt utterly bereft.

During that year away I wasn't afraid that the marriage would end. I felt very secure. I was well developed in my career, I knew where I was trying to go and the kids were a bit more independent. If it had happened I could have coped, whereas if it had happened ten years earlier I simply couldn't have. I wasn't looking for adventures; I was more intellectual and very, very busy. To completely relocate your family, your home, and a new set of workplaces is pure trauma. I don't get lonely and I've never been bored in my life. When I'm retired, if I'm here on my own I'll just go and sit on a rock down there and a whole new world will open up, or I'll read.

In Melbourne I moved from senior lecturer in art history to principal lecturer, but I was only principal lecturer for one year when the Dean retired. I'd written out an application form which I kept until four-thirty p.m. on the day that it closed and kept looking to see if a likely Dean had applied. I slipped mine in at five p.m. on closing day. I was not prepared to work under a twerp—I wanted to work under someone who would be really good. I was not ambitious for that position but ambitious for my ability to work without frustration. I felt I was a 'late bloomer'. One of the problems that women suffer is their own questioning of their ability, which they don't take for granted, whereas men do tend to take it for granted. I got the job.

So now the private passions and the public life began to come together. About that same time I was invited to become the Chair of the Visual Arts Board, and that was probably one of the most useful professional experiences I've had. I was four years with the Australia Council—one year as the Chair of the Visual Arts Board and then three years as both deputy Chair of the Australia Council and Chair of the Visual Arts Board, and that was really very important. More than anything else, that made me confident enough to become director of the Western Australian gallery, because we were dealing with exhibitions and artists and getting to know the whole of the contemporary Australian art world. Janet Holmes à Court suggested to her husband Robert, who was the Chair of the gallery board when Frank Ellis left in Western Australia, that I might be an appropriate replacement. He put a headhunter on the job who talked to a lot of people and I had an exhaustive interview with a headhunting firm in Melbourne. Then I heard nothing. The headhunters kept ringing me up and asking if I was still interested and I said I was. When it got to November I told them to forget it because I was beginning to think about the next academic year. A week later I got a phone call asking would I go over to the West. I decided I would and asked if this was for an interview and was told they were not sure but I should go. I had the whole day at the Art Gallery and met all the members of staff and the interview was for five-thirty in the afternoon. I went back to the hotel and 'dolled' myself up and got there at five-fifteen. I was wondering how I would handle this question or that question and was so engrossed that I looked at the clock and saw that it was six. I told myself not to lose track of my thoughts and was still thinking about how I'd deal with the interview. Next time I looked at the clock it was seven. Nobody had come out—they were all in the boardroom. I wondered whether I should stay on or slip away because they'd forgotten. I thought, 'No, blow it!' By seven-thirty I was a bit stroppy and thought, 'I'm going to sit here and when they finally come out I'll say, "Good evening, gentlemen. I've been here since five-thirty this afternoon, but I hope you had a good meeting!"' And just as I was thinking that and lost all of my train of thought someone emerged and asked me to come in. So in I went and Robert introduced me around the table in a fairly desultory way as if it wasn't of much import. I was beginning to think, 'Is this an interview? Perhaps it's not.' I sat down and he sat down and everyone was sitting there. And one of his famous long silences ensued. He used to use silence as a weapon. But I was still a little stroppy and I thought, 'I won't utter. If I have to sit here for three-quarters of an hour further I will not utter.' And the silence stretched on and on and in the end he suddenly turned his head and said, 'You'll be pleased to know you've just been appointed the director of the Art Gallery of Western Australia.' It completely swept the carpet from under me—but that was his *modus operandi*. I moved into that job feeling fairly confident because of the Australia Council, and brought the whole family with me. I went ahead to look for the house. I started off by renting and we put the stuff in storage, but then it took us a long time to find the house.

I left Perth because Robert really was a difficult person to work with. I would have been quite happy if I had been just working for him. But I also had responsibility to the minister, to the artistic community, to the general public, to the public service commissioner. He was a one-man boss and you had to show total and absolute loyalty and obedience, which I couldn't give because I was a public servant. I learned a lot from him and thought he was close to being a genius in his area of operation. Had he employed me in his Bell enterprises I would have worked perfectly happily with him.

They rang me about the director's job at the National Gallery in Canberra. A lot of people had looked at this job and thought, 'Oh, twenty-four years of James Mollison—what fool is going to take that on?' James had a preferred applicant, too, and he'd been really plugging him hard. First of all I said no when they asked me if I would apply. When I realised the Western Australian job was not going to work I rang back about ten days later and asked if the position was still open.

They said it was and to come over. I always discuss everything with Roy and he knew I was not happy.

Roy is still my best friend and he's the person that I most like to talk with. We can go off and drive for two days and just never stop talking because we've got the same interests. We are constantly feeding in to each other. How it would be if Roy wasn't a painter I don't know. It really is now an equal partnership.

So we decided I should take the job and moved to Canberra. I felt that the National Gallery had reached a point where it needed a real stir, and I know that's not an enviable thing to take on. I had a lot of trouble at the beginning with staff. Rumours were going around like 'unqualified', although I had qualifications probably better than anyone else in the place. Also 'inexperienced'—James had come to it from being director of the Ballarat gallery and I came to it from being director of a state gallery! 'A 58-year-old mother of four.' Well, imagine James Mollison being described as a 58-year-old father of none—give me a break! Even if I'd opted for the status quo it would have been hard. I think it's a fine and wonderful national facility, but I thought it was too inward turning. It was fashioning itself a bit on London's National Gallery, which is fine if you can sit on Trafalgar Square like Queen Victoria and the world will come to you. But the National Gallery here is sitting in a population of 300 000 in the centre of Australia. We can't sit here and complacently say we're the best. We simply have to put all of those taxpayers' dollars to very good effect, and that's been my aim. People making assumptions that because I'm a woman I'm not going to be able to cope make me cross. I thought, 'I will show you.' And I have shown them. And there is no doubt that the National Gallery is not only now well-endowed with federal money but is playing a national role in the exhibitions it brings into the country and the exhibitions it sends out, like Sidney Nolan to the Metropolitan in New York. I discovered that the salary bill was well in advance of what the government was paying and they had been topping it up in the past with the proceeds of exhibitions. In 1991 I could have no exhibitions and I had a salary bill in excess of $2 million over our government allocation and no way of making it up. That was when I did the first round of voluntary redundancies. That's not how you win friends and influence people. I've now got an exhibition development fund, and the gallery has mostly come around to my way of thinking.

Professionally this is the happiest I've been in my life. Personally I love this house that is designed for our needs. Roy and I don't have separate rooms or wings. I have never had a study or space of my own domestically. Roy has always had his studio. If I wasn't working I'd probably have to build a little room on for myself. I wouldn't like Roy and me to sleep in separate rooms, because first thing in the morning and last thing at night is when we do our talking. I leave for work at eight and am often not home before eight at night. But I am working at my private and public passion. I'm now working on a wonderful exhibition that will happen after I retire. I will have been there six years when I'm sixty-five and I think between six and eight years is the right amount of time to be in any one job.

I won't go back to painting, but I would hope to be

perceived as a useful person on boards and advisory areas. One of the things that Australia needs to do is project its cultural image to the rest of the world more effectively. I would love to be involved in something like that. I don't like to get into anything unless I feel I have an absolute contribution to make. It's all or nothing with me. And always will be.

Driving back along the country roads to the airport, I had a strong sense that despite the passion that she expressed when she talked about art, there was still a lot of emotion that was held in.

'Is it calm or a lifelong habit of control?'

She laughed. 'One of my mother's favourite sayings whenever I was rowdy or gave a bit of a whoop was, "Just because you are enjoying yourself, it doesn't mean you have to shout."'

I told her that when she does retire and become the next Governor-General of Australia, as the media is predicting, then I'll be the first to whoop and will encourage her to do likewise.

Part II

Juggling the Self

Gabi Hollows

Jerry Rogers

Ann Hollingworth

These three women, Gabi Hollows, Jerry Rogers and Ann Hollingworth, have led conventionally middle-class lives and married men who achieved great success and high public profiles in their fields. They have all juggled the various demands placed on them by their partners, their partners' careers and their children, with their own need for a sense of self. They took on the domestic responsibility of organising everyone's lives and keeping the home fires burning. They have all lived in very traditional marriages but maintained some sense of their own identity; no merging of selves has taken place.

Gabi Hollows had her own career alongside that of her husband. She saw herself as an equal partner, playing a vital role in their goals. Jerry Rogers took on renovating houses and real estate, but never felt that it was part of her identity. Ann Hollingworth had her own career as a physiotherapist when she married, and has maintained it on a part-time basis throughout her marriage.

Gabi Hollows stood up for herself against a very dominating, charismatic man. She did not take on the role of victim when he abused her for being stupid or incompetent, because she was confident that she was good at what she did. She also knew that the reasons for his disturbed reactions pre-dated his relationship with her. Jerry Rogers built everything around Bob, his career and their family. When she wanted to change the basis of their relationship, tension developed. Peter Hollingworth has always encouraged Ann to work and maintain her own profession. Both of them knew the importance of her having a life of her own, apart from their shared life.

These women believe that they are equal partners in their relationships. They are the anchors, the ones around which all else revolves, but they also insist on the fulfilment of their own needs. They have spent their lives juggling their own and others' needs in order to keep their marriages working.

Gabi and Ann established a pattern of behaviour in terms of their own work from the beginning. Jerry has tried to change the nature of her relationship with her husband when the patterns of their marriage were already established.

Gabi Hollows

Before Fred's death

The taxi dropped me off outside the imposing two-storey, grey stone former convent, now called Farnham House but better known as the residence of Australia's larrikin saint, Professor Fred Hollows, his wife, Gabi, and their five children. Their faces had smiled at me from the front pages of every major paper in the country as Fred Hollows received almost every prestigious award ever bestowed on an Australian doctor. The latest was the highest honour by Rotary International for World Understanding, and Fred Hollows was the first Australian to receive it.

Gabi opened the door. She was exactly like her photos: slim, youthful, attractive and warm. She smiled, shook my hand, led me into the house and introduced me to everyone. There was her brother, her five children and a friend, but she told me they often have at least six live-in house guests. The children didn't look too impressed with my presence—they must be sick of endless journalists, writers and film-makers invading their home to record their father's life, and by implication theirs.

There was a feeling of life and energy overflowing from one room to another. We moved into the engine room, the kitchen, where Gabi made me a coffee and answered several phone calls. She explained that Fred was in hospital, having just had a CAT scan that wasn't at all positive. Where the cancer used to appear like confetti, she told me in a matter-of-fact way, it was now resembling a snowstorm. They would all be visiting him later.

It became clear why Gabi talked very quickly and jumped from one topic to another with great rapidity. She was on 24-hour call and never knew what the next demand or who the next visitor would be. I found it very hard to keep her on the track of her own life.

After the interview, we waited outside on the front verandah for my taxi. I looked at the beds of brightly coloured petunias, which Gabi told me she planted for Christmas. A long wooden table with benches either side dominated the verandah. There had been sixty people there for Christmas, friends from different places and different races. Gabi said it had been a moveable feast because everyone had either brought something to eat or helped prepare food in the kitchen. My head swam at the mere thought, but Gabi clearly thrived on it.

New Year's Eve, however, she had spent mending clothes alone with the children, while Fred was off cavorting in the desert with his mates. She didn't resent the fact that it was probably his last New Year's Eve and he chose not to spend it with her and the children. She never placed pressure on him to restrict his own needs and desires.

She worked hard at creating harmony, admitting that she often had to mend bridges between Fred and other people. She often thought to herself, 'Now, why would he say that to that person?' and immediately moved in to smooth over the conflict or the hurt. She hated it when people were not speaking.

'Life's too short for that, don't you think?' she said, waving at the taxi to stop in front of the house. 'I'm sorry Fred wasn't here to meet you.'

'But Gabi, it was *you* I came to meet.'

SOMETIMES it seems as if I've spent most of my life with sick people. My father suffered from a heart valve disease and had his first cardiac surgery when I was eighteen months old. He was very sick, and they said it was me who kept him alive. I'd pop around the door and say, 'Hello, Daddy' and that way keep things hustling along. It's a bit like Fred with our kids.

My father then had two or three major heart operations and he didn't die until 1979 so he did very well.

I was born in 1953 when my mother was forty and my father a couple of years older. I was born on my sister's fourteenth birthday and she died when I was fourteen. I have a brother, Tim, who went away into the army so I grew up like an only child, but I was always surrounded by older people. My sister's death really affected me. I have a very vivid memory of being with her the night before she died. When she was expecting her first child she'd been very sick, after the floods in Lismore, and this sickness recurred when her third child was only one. She was in Newcastle Hospital and no-one thought of her as being a terminal patient. She actually got out of bed and dropped dead from a pulmonary embolism because she had been sitting around in hospital and not mobilised. It was a great shock because she was more like a mother to me than my own mother. A good friend of hers who was a nun died the day before and everyone consoled themselves by saying, 'They went up to heaven together.'

Both my parents were from Newcastle and they moved to the country to have a better lifestyle. We lived in Gosford on twenty-five acres of poultry farm and citrus orchard. It's an area called the Ridgeway which is the main route that links Terrigal and the Central Coast—and is very busy in summertime. My father was an engineer by profession, and thought he would turn himself into a bit of a farmer. He was from a very traditional family; his father was a solicitor and in his world a woman's place was firmly in the home. My mother was a trained psychiatric nurse and I think she would have loved to have worked after she married, but she never went back to nursing. She was a very strong, independent woman, but she had a major stroke nine years ago, and is now in a nursing home nearby. She's pretty vague and physically gradually fading away.

When I was two some kids next door took me in the pusher out into the paddock with the cows. One of the calves knocked me over. I went tumbling down the hill and ended up with a convergent squint. So I had my first visit to the ophthalmologist when I was two and eye surgery when I was three. It was an excellent result and full binocular vision was restored. I have very strong memories of my surgeon, Clem Walters. He's a lovely man who used to say, 'Here's my little Gabriella.' He and Fred are very good friends. I used to go regularly for checkups. I would see the orthoptist, which is what I now am. So I've always known about ophthalmology and orthoptics and remembered those early experiences whenever I speak to a patient.

When my sister died and my father had one of his bouts of surgery he decided he couldn't return to the farm. He went to work as a shipbuilding engineer in the state dockyard in Newcastle and my mother maintained the farm, which was a huge amount of work for her. My most vivid memory of Friday night was Dad coming home off the Newcastle train and giving me lots of chocolate.

When he had his next bout of surgery and my sister was first married we moved back to Newcastle during the week and came home to the farm on weekends. I spent lots of time with different groups of people. There were lots of kids and in those days it was safe to roam the roads. Our parents' farms were about a quarter-mile apart and we all rode ponies. When I turned five I went to the convent school. I had my Catholic friends, my public friends, my pony club friends and my girl guide friends. I've always been very gregarious.

I would have loved to have become a vet, because I loved animals and horses. Living in the country you often have those aspirations. I suspect, however, that I wouldn't have been academically serious enough to really pursue it. Traditionally in my family all the girls have boarded at the Dominican convent. I didn't want to do that because I was strongly involved with my pony club and a boyfriend, so I went to Gosford High School, but the change from an all-girls Catholic convent was a bit of a shock. At the convent we were used to saying, 'Good morning, God bless you, Sister,' then saying a few prayers and starting the lesson, whereas at high school the teacher would walk in and no-one would even speak to them or look up when they entered the room. But it had a good academic standard.

The day I finished my HSC I got a job at Gosford Hospital as a physio, helping people cough up and I really loved that. There was a lovely Canadian physio that we worked with and she was coughing up this old man who'd just come back from surgery and his sutures broke and all his intestines came pouring out. So I had a fun time. Although I had it in my head that I wanted to be a physio, I still went for the interview to be an orthoptist. The interview was really terrifying—suddenly there I was in front of the whole orthoptic board. There were about two hundred applications and they had to choose only eight people. They rang and said they were considering me but I had to make up my mind about physio. I chose orthoptics and that was that. I'd had visions of going to Sydney Uni and being with crowds of people, and I ended up at the Sydney Eye Hospital with a group of eight people. That's when I first came across Fred. My first optics lecture was at the Prince of Wales Hospital and he was taking one of the seven a.m. clinics. His first question was, 'Which one of you knows the optics of a slit lamp?' I was the only one brave enough to say, 'I don't know' and he said, 'Well, bloody well pull it apart and find out.' He was pretty ferocious and we were all shaking in our boots. I was eighteen and Fred was forty-three. I loved the Prince of Wales because you were really involved with the study alongside the registrars and the medical students. That's when I almost wished I'd done nursing, but we had a very intensive course over two years with lots of hands-on experience. Now it's a four-year degree course.

At this stage I was going out seriously with a guy called Lawrie who was a GP. In fact he only recently got married in our house. I like to keep in touch with all my former friends and lovers. It's much easier if everyone's friends. When I graduated I worked in Newcastle, then Gosford, and then I decided I wanted to see Sydney, so I started doing some locums at the Prince of Wales. This was 1975. Fred and I were working together. His first wife Mary had died in the June of '75.

My relationship with Fred got quite serious quite soon. A lot

of people think we met on the trachoma program but we didn't. I think Fred knew that this was coming up and that he had to have a woman to travel with. You can't go into a black camp being a single white fellow. But that wasn't his motive. We spent a long time together in Aboriginal camps working on their national trachoma and eye program and we worked well together.

Fred wasn't necessarily the greatest passion of my life, but I've always preferred older men. It might be because my father was so much older, but I think women are far more mature than men of the same age.

Fred is an overpowering, cantankerous person. Initially I had no idea that we'd ultimately end up together. There were many times when I thought, 'What am I doing here with bloody Fred shouting at me? Where's lovely Lawrie?' I've always been a very upfront person and Fred's like that, too. He can't stand people who are sulky and moody. He likes it all out front, and then it's over. That's what I'm like. I'm never shy with anybody and have no hesitation about expressing my opinion to whoever I'm talking to. I've never been scared of authority figures. I always stood up to teachers at school.

When Fred moved into this house, so did I. Because my parents were very Catholic and conservative I didn't tell them the details. I knew they'd say, 'What are you doing with this dirty old man, this Communist, this friend of Frank Hardy?' So what they didn't know didn't hurt them. I think these days things are very different. Fred kept saying to me, 'We've got to get married,' and I'd say, 'Well, maybe one day.' We'd done the trachoma program together, been in every black camp and worked together overseas really well as a team. People kept saying, 'When are you going to marry that woman, Fred?'

We were thinking very seriously about it when my father died. Then Fred's mother got very ill, and in fact died just before we got married. It was really sad. My parents and I got on very well with his parents when they came over from New Zealand. Everyone got along well together. In fact, my father first met Fred many years before I did. There was a Labor Party Conference in Terrigal in 1972 and Fred had gone for a jog. He'd come panting along our road and my dad was trimming the hedge. Dad said something like, 'G'day. Would you like me to get you a fresh orange juice?' Fred stopped and caught his breath while Dad squeezed him an orange drink and they had a chat. It wasn't until years later that they both remembered how they'd first met.

Anyhow, eventually one Sunday we drove up to my parents' place for him to ask them if it was okay to marry me. We had scones and jam and cream and he kept going to say it and stopping. Eventually he asked my mother in the car park before we caught the train.

I think I was a bit scared about finally going through with it. But I never thought his life would overpower mine. We had a firm base of other people living here with us. Fred and I were very much a team and very much together. So we had a wedding here with about 300 people, big jazz band, honeymoon, the whole works. It was great fun.

My feelings for Fred have never changed. His positive outlook and the way he just got on with life and did things were what attracted me most to him. My father had been brought up by the Jesuits and was incredibly careful and strict. He was always very cautious before he acted. My mother is the sort of person you go shopping with and she'll say, 'That's nice but you don't need it.' I liked Fred's impulsiveness. So I took the plunge and thought, 'One day I might be lucky enough to have a little baby' and now I have five little babies. Campbell, our son, was born in 1982. Fred was fifty-one and he was pretty pleased about it. When little Emma came along I thought, 'Now I've got one of each and that's perfect.' When Cam was nine months old we travelled overseas with him and when Emma was eighteen months old we went to Nepal. I still kept up my work at the hospital on a part-time basis until the others came along.

At home I've always been the front person for Fred, kept the kettle boiling, done the networking and the interacting. My job has always been preparing the patient for Fred, but that doesn't make me feel lesser. Even though he shouts a lot and says I'm an idiot and why don't I get my act together, I know he's all bark and no bite. He would never take on anybody he didn't consider competent. He always goes on about me being hopeless and useless, but I know in my deepest heart that he respects my ability to get on with things and get things done.

If Fred's in a bad mood, you don't want to be anywhere near him. He can be incredibly overpowering. We've had some huge fights. We've never thrown chairs but I've kicked him in the shins and felt like throttling him with his own socks. It doesn't matter who's there. I'll say exactly what I think and so will he. Neither of us bite our tongues so it happens a lot. They're open, clean fights. We hold no grudges. Basically I know how to sow a seed into his mind. Most partners know how to program each other. It's a good partnership.

Fred's not very tactful and he's not good at biting his

tongue. But when he gives people his full attention they feel as if they're his whole world. When he's with them he'll give everything; whether it's five minutes or five hours that they are with him he gives them 100 per cent absolute focused attention. That's why he's so good with his patients. His illness has made a change. He gets really upset that he can't do what he'd like to do. The fact that he can't just walk down to the shop, buy an ice-cream and walk back really pisses him off. We are very open about his illness, especially in front of the kids. We take each day as it comes. I think one of the reasons I've coped with it so well is my early experience of dealing with that and it's been a great source of strength.

All of the awards that he has received have been a great source of warmth and comfort to him. He feels very honoured and at times almost overindulged. But they are all very special to him.

I do envisage a life without him, but the most important thing is to maintain the momentum which has snowballed out of what's happened. I will absolutely commit myself to the work. In some ways I am more passionate about it. I want to bang a big drum and say, 'Come on!' Whenever Fred acknowledges anything that's been achieved he always acknowledges me. Anyone who knows Fred knows that I'm there beside him all the time. Apart from my role as a mother I am totally committed to providing the Third World with the same first-class care in ophthalmology as we have. If we can just prove that we can do it in three places—Eritrea, Nepal and Vietnam—it will show what's possible.

I know I have played a very important part in all the achievements. I don't think all this could have been achieved without me. People trust Fred because he's a mover and a shaker. They always say, 'Give Fred the money today and he'll spend it tomorrow.' The average Australian identifies with the

fact that Fred is like a bull at a gate; he just goes through it and says 'Bugger it!'

Fred may have had a go at being unfaithful early on but I've allowed him that freedom. I think basically he's been very satisfied in his own family unit and that's made him feel pretty special. I think people trust him because he's got that solid family base. We have had incredible support from the public. The Fred Hollows Foundation has raised over five million dollars, but it's been a real grassroots fund-raising campaign. We couldn't have done without every five cents that some little old lady has come and given us. That means as much to me as $500 or $5000 from some other person who can just write out a cheque with no worries. None of it could have happened without the support of all our friends and colleagues. We had over eighty ophthalmologists work with us on the trachoma program.

Sometimes it does all get a bit much and I'd dearly love to be living in a tiny solitary place with no children, no crazy husband and just be myself. But really I'm a very happy person. I'm angry about Fred being sick, but so is everybody else. When you go to a nursing home and see all those old people just sitting there waiting to die you can't help thinking about Fred and what a waste it is. Sometimes I think that Fred's being sick has made a lot of people act. Not that I'm writing Fred off yet; he's an incredibly strong person. He's also a very difficult person to deal with just in terms of time management. Sometimes when I'm on the phone he'll call out, 'Get off the phone—I want my dinner,' and I'll say, 'Shut up! I'm coming.' Yes, he is sexist, but he's also a 'now' man—'I want my dinner *now!* Where's my handkerchiefs?—*now!*' He's like that with everyone. I don't make a fuss about it. I just say, 'Use tissues!' I think a lot of his behaviour goes back to Mary and his own mother. If we move furniture and rearrange the room he goes bananas. A lot of times I wonder what happened in the past to cause this over-reaction. But I don't ask. I mean, that's him. You can't paint the spots off a leopard. It's like trying to tell Fred not to smoke. You're not going to change him. You have to accept people for what they are.

I keep explaining this to the children. Poor Cam gets a lot

of abuse from his old dad. Fred says, 'Why aren't you out riding a bike, you fat, lazy son—instead of watching TV?' If Cam goes and rides his bike, he says, 'Why aren't you reading a book?' A lot of it is Fred's anger that he can't do things with the kids that he'd like to. He loves having five kids and he thinks they're all wonderful. Sometimes I think I'd like to live in the country and get the kids horses. But I think

the kids have had a very enriched life with all the people they've been exposed to and the life they've led.

I just love having them all around, especially as I had no brothers and sisters around my own age. It's a crazy life but it's never boring.

After Fred's death

Like most people in Australia, I had seen photographs of Fred's memorial service and the subsequent funeral in Bourke. I had read the eulogies by well-known people, all attesting to Fred's great courage, strength and charisma even at the point of death. But what of Gabi Hollows?

When I rang to confirm the time for the interview Gabi said she had a streaming cold, and from the sound of her coughing it was probably worse than that, but true to her spirit of accommodation she insisted on my coming over.

I found her at home surrounded, as before, by children and

friends—some who were visiting and some who were staying. She was her usual smiling, warm, welcoming self. The house looked the same and felt the same in terms of energy. The phone never stopped ringing, people never stopped calling in and Gabi continued to talk to me, seemingly oblivious to the chaos, the disruptions and her nagging cough.

My friends were around a lot when Fred died. It was like being on pause or on hold; everyone wondering how long Fred was going to last. In terms of the work we were doing, in terms of the foundation, in terms of friendship, we were on triple pause, and triple hold, saying 'Maybe he'll have six months or six weeks or six days.' There was always that horrible question mark on top of us. I really had to go from day to day. When it comes to death some people can't see beyond that. They can't get away from thinking, 'What will happen when that person dies?' In terms of life and death and people sort of coming and going, I've had it before so I knew I would be able to move on. But there were things I couldn't do. I wanted him to sign a whole lot of books for the kids, but I couldn't bring myself to ask him to do it. It got to the stage where I thought, 'I just can't get him to do it.'

The people that went to Bourke for the burial with me afterwards have been around a lot since. I knew all those people would still be there whatever happened; I knew they would still love me, I would still have that support. I've been very lucky because I've got such a strong base of people.

Fred got very angry if someone had died and he hadn't had time to say goodbye, so he would never stop anyone coming to see him. No-one realised how many people we knew. Some people would feel comfortable and come, some people couldn't come, some people are still having trouble.

Hundreds and hundreds of people came to say goodbye.

People of all faiths, all ideologies, all ages, all classes. It was incredible. People flew in from all around the world. The most important thing for me with Fred was that I didn't want him to die in hospital. I wanted him to be at home. He was a person and we all loved him. I wasn't going to pack him up and say, 'We can't touch you.' The last official thing we had was the International Rotary Award and they did that at the hospital. That was exactly a month before he died. He was in hospital about ten days after that before he came home.

A friend, Paul, went to pick him up because he had to have some oxygen to get home. Fred was giving the nurses such a hard time. He was worried about how he would cope at home, whether he was going to be a burden on me, whether he was going to be able to handle it. Would the kids be able to handle it? I knew he wanted to come home so much but he didn't know if he could do it. I said, 'Look, forget it, I don't care. I can deal with anything. I don't need nurses. I've just got good common sense.' We put him in the front room downstairs. He said he would go out the back but I said, 'Bullshit, I don't want you back there in the house, I want you to be out the front. We can open the door, people can come and go and sit out on the verandah.' He was really worried about imposing on the household.

The only thing that worried me was the fact that my laundry never stops and it was right behind his room and when he had his oxygen going, the washing machine was buzzing away. I thought it might annoy him. That day was one of the hardest of his life. It was just like bringing a new baby home.

I felt okay about it. The kids accepted it. They had a broken old teddy or dolly or a bird with its wing fallen off. But Anna said to me, 'Mum, if Dad wasn't a person, you would want him to be out of his misery.' And that was really honest. You wanted him to be there forever, but you didn't want him to be there for too long. I had always wanted him to be around for the twins' birthday and the day that Anna started school, which was the day he had his kidney out. The day he finally came home to die I have never seen him so cross. Everyone was scared of him. It was okay as far as I was concerned, but we didn't know how long it was going to go on. As time went by it resolved itself. When you love somebody and you don't want to let go of them you want to smother them with love and get really close. Is it harder to do that or easier to be a bit more withdrawn in terms of your real emotions?

I had lots of very conflicting thoughts. I really wanted to smother him but I had to be incredibly bossy and say, 'Shut up, Fred. Go and have a shower.' I can't stand bad nursing. He would say, 'I'm not going to have a shower now, don't boss me around.' I had to be incredibly clinical about it, and treat him as though he was just a patient. The day before he died he was really cranky with me and I just burst into tears and left the room. I couldn't help it. I had this big howl. The doctor said, 'You've just got to remember he's dying. We are doing the best we can for him and he is not himself. He is not really in control of how he wants to be.' He'd just been with a patient who was dying, whose family had just taken him to the hospital and left him there. They had wanted him to be at home but he'd been fighting with his wife and his son all day in the same sort of situation. All we could do for Fred was make him comfortable. It was very hard to have that sort of abuse from him because it was all anger against the end. It was very hard to cope with that as well.

The day he died we had been going for twenty-four hours straight. Someone was with him all the time. Clarrie had checked himself out of hospital to be with Fred. Clarrie was Australian light-heavyweight champion in the Fifties and Fred would tell you he had broken more police jaws than any

Aboriginal in Australia. Clarrie died three weeks after Fred died. It was almost as if Clarrie needed to be up there to give Fred a hand. Clarrie was this solid presence that was there constantly. The college blokes rang and wanted to present Fred with a medal and I said, 'You'd better come now because I don't think he's going to be here tomorrow.' I didn't know it was going to be his last night, but I had that feeling.

The people who were there for that last night were very special people. Even when he was sleeping and talking in his sleep, I just wanted to listen. He didn't stop, his mind was just amazing. I just wanted him to be in control. It was pretty heavy when it came to the crunch. The last ten minutes.

I was asked if I wanted the children around and I said, 'Of course I want them around.' The children were wonderful. We even joked a bit. One of the children made a rocket, which went in the coffin with Fred, together with a bottle of whisky. All the kids were strong. Inner strength is something I knew I had. Everyone seemed to get Fred's energy, not just me.

After the funeral and the burial I didn't want to go anywhere. I went to Vietnam at the end of March but only for a week. That was a really hard thing to do, but I knew I had to carry on the work we had started. The children stayed with friends and I took off with the team. It was the right thing to do. Fred would have wanted it. Vietnam gave me a lot of strength. Every person I met I would have loved to have brought back with me. Every person we dealt with must have had some personal tragedy, but they were just getting on with it. People like that are so strong, and that gave me an amazing feeling. I don't want any more than I've got. I haven't got Fred, and that's really hard, but I don't think Fred wanted us to sit around and be sorry for him. There is a sense of relief that he wasn't discomforted and in more pain.

There's one side of me that says I just want to stay and not talk to anybody and just be Mum. There's another side that's incredibly professional and can't begin to think of the surgeons and ophthalmologists not having the opportunity to do what I know they need to do. They are so patient in terms of what we do—in three countries on three different continents with huge differences in populations. There is another side that says I would like a holiday, but then I forget about it.

Lots of people have said I have to slow down or I'll be dead. There is no way I couldn't personally be doing what I'm doing, because I've been so much part of it. I couldn't just sit back. There is more pressure now, of a different type. Fred wasn't an easy person—there was lots of tension, so that side of it is now not with me. The other side of loss is really hard. I always wonder, 'What would he say about this?' or 'What would he do?' or 'How would he make a decision?' I can't feel in terms of the work we are doing that we can just trade on Fred's name. I have to be there, in order to maintain that quality that he had about everything.

I do believe in fate and I do believe that one door shuts and another one opens. I'm obviously not meant to be a nun, and I don't want to spend the rest of my life by myself. I'm not going to be a merry widow, but I think that the person who ends up with me could only understand if they had known Fred. It's a funny feeling, but I know someone is out there. I'm forty, and I don't want to go charging into relationships, but it would be good to see down the track. Fred used to say to me, 'I might not be your only husband, but by God I'll be the best looking one.' The hardest part of my life now is not pushing myself too hard.

The most important thing for kids is that they have a base. I don't want to go off and have a holiday by myself. I want to have it with my kids. In terms of the Hollows Foundation it is a really important time—a knitting-together time. I'm certainly not trying to step into Fred's shoes. I feel very comfortable doing what I'm doing, because I really do know what I'm talking about. I've been right beside him the whole way. It wasn't just Fred who did things by himself; it was always a team effort. We have to give people the confidence that it's still the same—we won't have Fred but we will have his conscience. As Fred always said, 'There's only one way of doing something and that's the right way, and that's what we're trying to prove.' I have to somehow keep it all together and keep everyone on course—the kids, the foundation, the team and myself. I'll give it my best and I won't give up.

After the interview, I left with other friends who lived near where I was going. In the car we talked not of Fred, but of Gabi. They told me how incredibly strong she has been and is still. They expressed their great admiration for her ability to cope with all the conflicting demands.

'Little Gabriella' now has not only her five children and the Fred Hollows Foundation to maintain and sustain, but also the Hollows team of surgeons and helpers. She will have to juggle all their needs as well as her own. It's a daunting legacy.

Jerry Rogers

Although I had known of Bob Rogers as a star of television and radio, it was Jerry whom I came to know well. I have known Jerry for more than ten years and often stayed at Jerry and Bob's home in Mosman. One day when I was there discussing this book with Jerry, I suddenly said, 'This is all about you. These issues are the very topics you have been discussing for years. You should be in the book.' Convinced of the truth of this argument, Jerry agreed. It is difficult to interview formally a close friend with whom you have exchanged all your own thoughts and feelings, but I knew that Jerry's journey as a woman was an important one.

The Jerry I had known was always beautifully groomed, poised, well organised, incredibly calm and in control of her life. And yet I knew from our talks and the books she read that she was on a journey that some would call 'spiritual'. It was a journey in which she hoped to discover what was true for her. And it hadn't been an easy path.

Before we began the interview she showed me the wonderful paintings she had recently completed which had been giving her so much joy. I could see from her face that her discovery of this source of creativity in herself had given her a whole new sense of being alive. Her visual talents had always been evident in the way she had decorated the house, the way she placed food on a plate, the way she designed her garden or put flowers in a vase, but never before had I seen a painting of hers. Now the sunroom was full of them and her face was shining.

I met him on a blind date. It was a bitterly cold Hobart night in March, and I remember all I had on was a white organdy blouse and a black silk skirt, and high heels. Crazy now when you think of it, but that's how women dressed in the Fifties.

It was love at first sight. We were engaged in April and married in June. In those days if you wanted sex you had nowhere to have it, so you got married. The last thing my father would have accepted was my marrying a Catholic or becoming pregnant out of wedlock. In later years, as I learned more about my father, I discovered his problem was that he was an illegitimate child. He never told any of us and that was his shame. He did not want his only daughter to bring that sort of shame on the family.

As an only daughter with five brothers I grew up in a very competitive environment where, if I was to be accepted by my brothers, I had to be as good as they were in most things. I had to wrestle as well as they could, play cricket as well as they could—and the great legacy was that I was a very happy child. It was a poor childhood in the 1930s with six kids on a basic wage in Townsville, northern Queensland, but my mother let me run wild with the boys. Looking back now, I know that what has been the greatest strength in all my life is the fact that I knew my mother really loved me. I was the only girl and the jewel in the crown, but she did not try to protect me, she just let me roam free. To grow up being loved gives you the confidence to do what you want to do. Unconditional love is the greatest gift that you can be given.

When I was fourteen and a half, my mother had a major operation and I was at a commercial high school learning shorthand, typing, bookkeeping. After her operation she needed to be looked after for a few months, so I left school and never went back. After that I went into my first job. In those days all the children helped keep the family going. If you earned thirty-five shillings a week you gave your mother thirty shillings a week and had five shillings for your fares and whatever. So the more children who could go to work earlier, the better.

When I was sixteen I was having a tough time with my father, in the sense that being the only daughter, he did not want to let me out of his sight. I

found out that I could leave home legally as long as I could support myself. When I was seventeen, I wanted to go around the world and my father said, 'I will let you go as long as you don't go to Sydney, because that is a pit of evil.' I said, 'All right, I will go with my friend Daphne and we will start going around the world by going down to Tasmania.' So we went to pick raspberries in the hills behind Hobart. We lasted six weeks. After being chased by snakes and God-knows-what we came out with twenty-five shillings between us.

We went back into Hobart to stay at the Salvation Army girls' hostel, which was very respectable. I decided I did not want to go back into an office; I wanted far more freedom. Wrest Point had just opened and we applied for jobs as waitresses as it was a premier hotel in Australia. Bob was broadcasting on 7HO; he was twenty-two and he had been working in country stations.

My father had been a drover and became a butcher; my brothers were car salesmen. One brother particularly showed promise; he was a Communist at eighteen but he was killed during the war. So for me radio was a glamour occupation. I was used to men who did not show their feelings and when I met Bob he was very demonstrative, affectionate and loving. I had never experienced such openness from the men in my family. They were tough Queenslanders where men never cry. I met a type of man I had never known.

I didn't think about my future—I was so overwhelmed by falling in love that I would have given up anything. It was a wonderful courtship; most of the love songs he played at night on the radio were for me. I listened every night and it was a wonderful fairytale. Our first home was a gardener's cottage at the back of a wonderful huge old colonial house.

My mother was married at eighteen, my grandmother was married at eighteen, and all I was doing was following the pattern. I was working as a receptionist in Heathhorn's Hotel; later, when we went to Melbourne, I worked for a hearing aid company and when we went back to Brisbane I had a similar job.

I was absolutely, totally, over-the-moon happy. In Melbourne, when Bob was out of radio, he worked at the Tax

Department and hated it. Back in Brisbane he gradually went back into radio on 4BH; he had a half-hour or so on Sunday. He found the sponsors, was paid per session and gradually built up an audience. I became pregnant and had my first child before I was twenty. In those days you stayed home after that; you had your children and you looked after your husband, which was what I did.

After our first daughter was born I started modelling, which was a glamour career at that time for any good-looking girl. I continued that after the birth of my second daughter when I was twenty-three, and when I was twenty-seven we came to Sydney for Bob to further explore his radio career.

My mother always said to me, 'Have a bit of money that your husband does not know about; I call it my running-away money.' A lot of women had this little bit that's put aside that the husband does not know about. I followed her advice.

I have always managed the money because my mother always managed the money. If it had been left to my father it would have gone on horses. I don't gamble because I saw the problems it created early in my own family. A couple of my brothers were bookmakers. My father held a book in Townsville at the dogs.

By the time Bob and I came to Sydney we had a substantial deposit because we had established what became a pattern, which was to buy a property, do it up and sell it at a profit. It was one way I saw of making money, being able to afford something better without actually having to go to work. In Brisbane we bought a wooden house high up on the slopes of Hamilton overlooking the Brisbane River. I had always been attracted to living with a view of water and it was an old wooden house which we gradually brought right up to the best we could make it. Before we came to Sydney we sold it at a great profit.

We both worked very hard on that house. I can remember pulling out thousands of copper nails for hours in the sitting room because the wallpaper had been placed on hessian and the hessian had been kept in place by copper nails. We spent probably nine months on that one room. It was tedious work but we didn't mind at all. I had four miscarriages between the first two children and the second two. So I was pregnant a lot of the time. When I saw how many divorces occurred with radio and TV personalities I was determined that my marriage would work. That was partly the reason for having more children, because we both adored our children and I thought they would bind the marriage closer together, which it did.

I tried to plan the pregnancies, but you ask almost anyone in that era—if the Dutch cap was not in correctly then you were pregnant. I seemed to be always pregnant. But because our sexual relationship was so good I felt that whatever child came out of it had to be a very wanted child.

Bob became a very attractive sex idol and he was out there amongst it all with enormous temptations. What man doesn't succumb to some of them? They are human. I tried to look at the situation from the long term and the number of people involved. I looked at the four children and knew that if they were to have a stable and happy home life, then I couldn't spend all my time worrying about whether my husband was being faithful or not. I didn't forget about it—it was always there—but for the peace of mind of the whole family, I accepted the situation. I had many opportunities not to be faithful, but it is not my nature. If I make a bargain, it's like a contract: I keep it. I don't think it was his nature to be unfaithful; I think he is a very loving and giving man. But man is a different animal.

I did not have positive evidence of his infidelity and I did not seek it out. One always hears things, one way or another, but whatever Bob did outside of the marriage he never brought it home and he was absolutely totally discreet. I think he really loved me and he loved the family and I think whatever happened with other women was not meaningful or long term. Flattery played a big part—lots of women throwing themselves at him. I am not defending him, but it's realistic, it's life.

I thought it was a very good marriage, and sexually it was terrific. People underestimate the sexual bond because when you really relate to one another sexually there is a spiritual quality in it that is quite wonderful. Ours was always written up in magazines as a glamorous life. It was the time of the big night clubs, like André's and Checkers, and there was an opening night every week. There were always top personalities coming in for the opening, so you were expected to front up and look very glamorous; it was part of the role. So I dressed up, smiled, played the part, but my heart wasn't in it. I went along with it as Bob's wife, but neither of us made any lasting friendships out of it.

I tried not to have the children publicised because they had enough troubles being children of a very well-known personality. It did affect their growing up and I tried to keep the press away from them as much as I could. In the playground they were known as the children of a well-known personality on radio and television, and were often scapegoats for other children's jealousies and false friendships. It wasn't easy for them.

When we moved to this house in Mosman, which is on three street corners, we often found people circling the house. In the last twenty-three years I have screened us in very well, with trees and shrubs. We had one sponsor who used to circle this house every Sunday, wanting to be a part of our inner circle. That is one of the reasons we bought the farm in Queensland; it was a long way away and there are thirty acres. No-one can get close in.

Bob's career was successful; he was making lots of money, but he did not have the time to invest it. I started doing what I had done before, buying and selling houses, but on a much larger scale. It was a very exciting time; you could buy whole streets during the Seventies. I bought a street in Chippendale and had thirteen houses at one stage. I had a team—a carpenter, a plumber, an electrician and a painter—and I would move the team from one area to another. We would buy old houses and restore them, let or sell, refinance, and buy another one. Then I moved from buying houses to buying buildings. I stayed with it for a long time, and then I became bored. It was just a routine thing that anyone could do as far as I could see.

You needed the initial capital, but after that it just rolled on because you refinanced and went on to the next one. One day I snapped.

I have always been a fanatical gardener because I've found that the garden is the place where I can become restored. If I am down or desperate or even just for my everyday pleasure, I walk into my garden every day of my life and do something in it. I remember one day so clearly. I was in the garden, I was forty-two. Bob was working with me and I suddenly just sat down and started crying. He came over to me and said, 'What's the trouble?' I said, 'Is this all there is?' It sounds so corny now. Bob did not understand what I was saying; in fact, I did not understand myself. I just knew that I wanted something more, much more. Bob said to me, 'You have got everything a woman could want.' In a way he was right, but what I hadn't done was explore another side of me which had been hiding a long time. There was a huge part of me that was empty.

When we first came to Sydney I tried to go to night school to do my Leaving. I had two children and Bob had just started on radio between six and eight at night. The hours were impossible and I knew I would have to wait until a later stage. Soon after I had that weeping session in the garden, I knew I needed to change direction.

It was the Whitlam era, so I went back to school. The Labor government had encouraged and enabled women to go back to further education, so three days a week I would walk from Mosman over to Seaforth Tech. I did my Leaving with a lot of other women, all mature age, and from there I went on to Macquarie Uni and did my BA. If I had failed during my Leaving it would have been devastating for me, because I was searching out an identity for myself. Up until that time my identity had been locked in with Bob and his career and making sure he and the family were successful. I wanted the kids to have everything materially, practically, spiritually—as much as I could give them. What I had not realised was that I was not getting what I needed for my own growth. I had not even thought about it. From the outside I looked as though I had everything—overseas travel, plenty of money, four beautiful children, a very successful husband, beautiful home, beautiful properties—but there was this emptiness. I was also a bit disgusted with myself for keeping on buying and selling property. I did not like some of the ethics around those things in which I was involved. After six years at university I came through with an honours degree in political science.

I started studying English but I gravitated towards history because I really wanted to know who I was, where I came from, what had shaped me. I felt I had to know Australian women's history and in particular the history of women from the time I was born.

Through history, and particularly through the feminist

courses, I learned so much about myself. My consciousness became so much more aware—raised, as they say. When I looked back on my life I realised that I had been half asleep. From that time onwards my marriage became quite rocky. When I started going to school and university my youngest daughter at the time was about twelve, and as I did not get home until 3.30 p.m. some afternoons Bob would pull the old stunt of the 'latchkey child'. He pulled every stunt he possibly could to stop me progressing in the way I wanted, because he was suddenly not the centre of my attention any more. I had moved him over to the sidelines and he did not like it. As time went on I moved him further to the sidelines, because I found that the lifestyle that I had shared with him, particularly going out for dinners and all of that, was out. There was no time for it any more and I did not want it. That was his lifestyle, not mine; mine became a very studious one. I talked to him about it but I don't think he ever heard the words, really. When men read words, they seem to read a different text to women. I find you can say things to women and women know immediately what you mean. You can say the same words to a man and he has no comprehension of what it is you are saying. Men and women come from two different species—they're elephants, we're horses. I don't think he heard much of what I was saying at all. He still wanted to be the centre of my existence. He didn't want anything to change. He still doesn't.

Bob was very, very threatened. I was going my own way and he certainly wasn't going to follow me. The number of divorces in mature age women students at Macquarie was large. Very well-educated men, like airline pilots, were tearing up their wives' notes before exams so that they wouldn't get through. There were so many extraordinary examples of threatened men. We all talked about it. Bob hated it so much that at one stage he left for six months. I must say, his new image did not show a great style. The red sports car, the Paddington pad with Italian furniture were a bit clichéd. I knew what it was about, but I also knew that we had a lot of unfinished business and that our marriage was not over. I felt I had to stay and be responsible and reliable for the family. His going in many ways did not inflict much discomfort because I had a very good separate income from the restaurant I owned.

I could not have risked giving in to him. My psychological survival as a person was at stake. I would have been very sick had I not continued the way I was going. I would have been no good for anybody. When I was going to university my third daughter was doing arts at Sydney University and we shared a lot of the study notes because she was also doing feminism. They understood where I was at and why I needed to do it.

Bob left for about six months, but I did believe he would be back. And he was. We had a bit of drama over the youngest daughter, who was having problems. You don't have those sort of disruptions in a family without creating a lot of disarray. She was at a very vulnerable teenage period, and she was a catalyst, really, in bringing us back together. I think that's been one of the primary roles in her life. The kids' well-being is of greater importance to us than our individual destinies; it always has been the case. Bob loves his children.

I suppose he may have thought that I would plead with him to come back, but there is no way I could have. I would have betrayed myself utterly. I would have liked his support and interest right through that university period, but I really did not get much of his interest. I understood why he was threatened, but I could not let it stop me going on, because I knew if I let his needs overcome my own needs I would have eventually been psychologically very ill.

The real war began when he returned, because we had to learn to live with one another and accommodate the different areas that we wanted for ourselves. It's not always easy, but I think we both realised that there is a lot going for us being together and staying together. The problem is that I had changed and would continue to change, and Bob had remained fixed.

Many times I would like to have left, but my children were always far too important to me. I would never have thought of taking the children away. I thought they were better off with their lives left undisturbed as much as possible in a familiar environment. I never contemplated uprooting them. Of course, they were aware of our conflict and they had some problems as a result of it, but then who ever gets off scot-free?

My eldest daughter is happily divorced; the second one is reasonably happily married, the younger two, twenty-eight and thirty, have not married but they are products of the younger generation who tend not to marry. They have seen me fight so hard to get an equal relationship and to get respect for myself as an individual, someone who is separate from, not glued to a man. The result is that they demand an equal relationship right from the start. Their sense of identity is not centred on a man; their identity is centred on their own abilities, their work, who they are. They are central, they don't make a man central, whereas my generation was taught that you were there for the man. When a man came home you were freshly showered, perfumed, the house was impeccable, the kids were clean, the meal was on the table. The whole centre of a woman's life revolved around the man. I tried that life for many years.

I am gratified to see that their identities are very firmly lodged within themselves and their abilities. A man is important to them, sure, for emotional, sexual and other reasons, but not economically and not for their sense of self-worth. That is the very big difference between my generation and my children's generation.

Women who never had the chance to go to university even now go all through their lives with this lack of self-esteem. It's a problem with men and women, but far greater with women. Without that sense of self-esteem you can achieve nothing.

I was practical. I realised that without economic freedom, you could have no other form of freedom. How can you separate yourself from the man or make any decisions unless you are economically free? Money is valuable for many things, but the very vital thing is choice; it gives you choice.

The degree for me was an exploration of self; I did not do a degree to get a job. I had plenty of jobs. I had a restaurant, now the Macleay Street Bistro, which I ran for five years; I had a tomato farm in northern New South Wales; I had a farm in Queensland; I was looking after other properties. It was pretty full on and I was employing a lot of people.

Now Bob has more and more accepted the fact that I am a different person, that I don't think the way he does, and my preferences in many areas are very different from his. This is a process; he is coming to accept the fact that I am entitled to a different way of life. Bob's enjoyments, like most men, are football, having a game of tennis and cards, whereas I'm not interested in any of those things. I am interested in painting, writing books, exploring craftwork, swimming, farming, growing things. It has been a very hard struggle and it still is, to get and keep that space. Bob was of a generation where, having expected to be central to a woman's life, he has not enjoyed being put to one side. Feminism has changed both our lives, but particularly his, and like most men he has bucked and kicked all the way. He is still bucking and kicking. I hope he is beginning to realise that not being central not only gives me freedom but it takes a lot of pressure off him.

Cooking and having a well-run house are still important to me and always will be because they are the basic pleasures of life. When you cook a beautiful meal every night, it's a great offering of love, and when you do a vase of flowers or you change a room around it gives pleasure to everybody, including me. Just because you change in one direction doesn't mean that you give up those things that you have always considered worthwhile; you simply add other things.

A lot of the meaning in my life comes from relationships, and if my relationships with those I care about around me are not good, I don't feel good. What more could a person want out of life than that your children become your best friends, that you share their interests, they share yours, and that you have a continuing and continual meaningful, rich dialogue? They are all cooks, gardeners, and involved in artistic and creative pursuits.

My mother was a fantastic role model, and I realise it more and more as I get older. She was a chambermaid when she was fourteen, married at eighteen, brought up six children on the basic wage, from which she had to save. She started to buy a house and then another house. If it had been left to my father, we would have been well entertained—he played the harmonica and the violin and the piano—but as I said he was a bit of a gambler. She had a fairly happy and sexually rewarding relationship with my father, but when he died after a fairly long illness of five or six years she was like a canary let out of a cage. It was quite an eye opener, because I saw this woman, whom I thought was reasonably happy within the marriage, suddenly blossom. She bought herself a bright yellow sports car and at seventy-three she whisked around the Tallebudgera Valley. The speed she drove at was unbelievable; we used to hold our breath as she went down the driveway. If you did not ring her for a week or so and you couldn't get her, she had probably gone to China, or Alaska, or Russia. She wasn't sitting around waiting for her children to ring. She was really quite an amazing woman. She did it all on her own. I think by that time she'd had enough of men. After five sons and my father, I think that she was going back to girlhood, to how she was at eighteen, before she was married.

I think I am getting to that stage. I promised myself I was not going to wait to seventy-three to do what my mother did. I have aimed to do the things I want to do within my marriage and that has been a struggle. To get Bob to change is like having to break both his arms, both his legs and almost every finger. I want independence and freedom but I still want this relationship. If I did want to go to China or Alaska, I would have to get the domestic ground in order. If he came with me he wouldn't like it, because he doesn't like going anywhere where he can't understand the language. Whereas one of the joys of my life is to go somewhere where you don't know what to expect.

Did you see the series 'Brain Sex', which showed how men and women's brains are different shapes and sizes and how in women, the left and the right side relate far more? I do believe that our brain structures are different. Whether this is genetic or whether it's the way we have developed, I don't know. All I know is, communication at any deep personal level is extremely difficult.

A lot of people comment on my state of calm. I think you earn calm, like you earn knowledge from reading a Patrick White novel. You have to work at reading Patrick White, and you also earn any calm or still centre. Over the years I have cried a lot. I could not have survived forty-four years of this marriage without a lot of turmoil and a lot of stress. I discuss what I care about with my close women friends. Women are terribly important to me—far, far more important to me than men. We discuss relationships all the time because they are fundamental to our lives, like my garden.

When I got my honours degree, I did not know whether to go on to do a PhD, but I sensed in a way I had reached the end of the road. I could go being an external student, but I did not want to do that either.

For a few years I really concentrated on the farm in Queensland. I became a member of the Rare Fruits Council and started an orchard growing exotic rare fruits. This occupied me for a few years and it still does, because I want to grow fruit organically. I'm ecologically very aware of what's happened to the environment, but I do love to try new flavours. It just extended an area where my daughter, who is a cook, can try experimenting with new fruits which are unknown, and develop new recipes. I grow them; she can cook with them. I've also got chooks, rare birds, and white peacocks. It's such a joy to see these creatures around you.

For thirty years I have been interested in the arts and crafts and artisans. In the 1970s I started collecting and commissioning pieces from different artisans whose work I really loved, mostly wall hangings. Collins Publishers approached me about doing a book on Australian knitwear designers, which I did, called *The Art of Knitting. A Sense of Place,* my second book, is based on Australian embroidery. This year I am considering writing a book called *The Bend of the River*—an anecdotal compilation of our life at the farm for the past twenty-five years and the richness it has given all of us.

I realised well after I finished the degree at university that mine was a spiritual as much as an educational search. I don't particularly come from a religious family but like everybody we need a philosophy in which to base our lives. I started reading Jung; I am still reading Jung. I think he is a goldmine for anyone who is searching spiritually. Now I am coming more and more to take each day as it comes, to roll with things. I am not searching as hard as I was.

My sixties and seventies are going to be very good because I can at last be who I am and who I want to be. I am that young, adventurous girl, but much more, because I've got all those years of experience and learning, knowing and hearing. In those past years, two of the most traumatic occurrences were an anorexic daughter who nearly died and a bulimic daughter who also nearly died. We have only spoken out about these things publicly recently, because one doesn't want to highlight those particular children, or invade their privacy. But they're old enough now for us to be able to discuss it without really upsetting them or their lives to any degree.

Bulimia and anorexia are common in high-geared upper-middle-class families who strive for excellence and are upwardly mobile. We were a classic case, and two out of our four daughters suffered in this way. We were a close family, and wondered what on earth we had done that was wrong. Experts still don't have any answers for anorexia or bulimia, but I think that being a perfectionist is not good for anyone. You only need to be perfect if you don't have great self-esteem.

Not everyone gets over anorexia or bulimia, and a lot of women carry it to the ends of their lives, but thankfully both girls have grown through it.

It is the sensitive, vulnerable ones who succumb. They were hard times because we kept it secret. Bob was very much in the public eye and we did not know what it was until our daughter had a major suicide attempt at twenty-one and nearly succeeded. I am eternally grateful that we did get through and get over it, because if one of them had died, I would have considered myself the greatest failure in the world. Nothing would have brought back my self-esteem. I would never have recovered. Neither would Bob. We would have considered any other success nothing, if anything had happened to our girls. I ask them now why it happened, and they say, 'I still don't know,

Mum.' Most children go through a period where the parents are always wrong, but when they mature they realise that you can go through the rest of your lives blaming your parents but finally you're the one who has to set things right. Ultimately you are responsible for your own destiny.

I think we made a mistake by giving them everything we did not have ourselves. They weren't allowed enough challenge on their own. I now realise I denied them struggle, and I accept that. We did it for all the best motives, but with my grandchildren I will never make that same mistake. I will never make it so easy. I'll allow them to struggle in their own right. You take so much away from a person when you don't allow that. We gave them everything. If they wanted something we opened a door. It was so wrong; it was overindulgence; it was a huge mistake. But coming from the backgrounds we came from it was probably understandable.

My mother had set me on a path that said to make money was to be successful. I don't despise that, because money gives you many paths and many choices, but you have to learn when to stop. If money becomes your god you are trapped.

When you know you have enough you should move on into other areas which provide you with quality in your life.

The problem is that my children, having always had money and the things it provides, are not too good at making it. It's the old story: if you haven't had to make it, you don't necessarily become entrepreneurial.

Bob had a very successful, very public career. For much of that I was the woman behind the successful man. I don't think he would have been so successful without me. I took charge of everything, emotionally and financially. I did all the organisation to make his life easy. His job was tremendously demanding and he gave everything he had. Whatever spare time or energy was left over, he gave to the family. I do believe, in that era particularly, that every successful man had a willing woman like me behind him. That's why it was so hard for women to achieve in their own right. If they were married their role was to provide the support for their husband and his career and if they were single then they didn't have all the benefits of a devoted wife. They didn't have someone at home shopping, cooking, washing, ironing. I always laid Bob's clothes out on the bed for him. Now he does his own ironing.

After being at the top in radio and television, Bob wanted to prove to himself that he could be successful in business. He is quite extraordinary in that other men of his era still need that ego boost; they are still behind the microphone even though they are multi-millionaires. Now Bob is thinking about retiring from the rag trade and returning to low-key radio, just for fun. He will probably die in front of a microphone. And why not? You meet far more interesting people in radio than the rag trade.

My latest and all-absorbing passion is my painting. I have taken to it like a duck to water and wished I had started when I was eighteen. Now I want to write and illustrate my own work.

My art teacher has freed me. I had been going to classes for a year and was not making the breakthrough I had hoped. Suddenly she showed me a technique that freed me and now I can't stop. I want to paint all day, every day.

I could never face that blank sheet of paper; it was probably like the blank page for a writer. So now I get a number of different inks and really mess up the page. Once it's messed up I abstract from it all kinds of different images. I have paintings of chooks, ducks, waterfalls, beaches. I can't tell you how much joy it's given me to see it all emerging before my eyes. It's like the sculpture that's in a piece of stone; suddenly you see it emerging. I did sculpture at Sydney Tech for a short period and loved it, but at that stage didn't have the time to pursue it.

When my youngest daughter started learning classical guitar I would take her to lessons. I was sitting there waiting and I thought, 'I might as well take lessons at the same time.' She and I learned classical guitar for about eight years. It's wonderful to have a house full of music, particularly home-made music.

I no longer think in terms of years; I simply enjoy the day. It's taken me a long time to arrive at this point in my life and I'm not giving it up for anything. Bob still resents the fact that I have changed so much from the girl he married. We are still engaged in a battle of wills, and apart from a shared interest in the family we don't share much else these days. Even if we decide to go and have a cup of coffee together, we can't agree on which path to take. I go my way and he strides off on his and we meet at the coffee shop. It's an ongoing battle.

I can't force him down my path and he can't force me down his. We are fair opponents who, when we meet on common ground, can have a very good time. He is a delightful travelling companion; nothing is too much trouble. I never try to drag him to the art gallery because he would be bored stupid.

So somehow we are still here, side by side. When you have known someone for a long time you know his good qualities and you know you are not going to agree with a lot of what he says and some of what he does, but you also know that when the chips are down he will be there. And the same is true for him with me. But I don't know if it's enough to keep a marriage going forever.

I suppose like lots of other wives I could have been traded in, like trading in the old car and buying the new one. It's a common story. I know our marriage would certainly have broken down had I not gone about evolving the way I did. In saving myself, I think I saved our marriage. We would both have been bored with it, and I would have been sick. I remember that book *The Yellow Wallpaper*, where a woman lacked a sense of identity and went mad. That's exactly what would have happened to me. I would have just been Bob Rogers' wife to the end of my days and that isn't what I wanted. I wanted to be a person in my own right and I also knew that money wasn't the answer to my problems. If you pay attention to what's going on within yourself, you feel it; you know that you're going down the wrong path. You have to stay in tune with yourself and be honest about how you are feeling. And then you have to act. You have to take the plunge to achieve the kind of life you really want and need. Sometimes it's very tough, but otherwise you will lose yourself. And then you've lost everything.

Before I left, Jerry showed me a poem by the American writer Raymond Carver, written just before he died. It's a poem that asks if you have got what you wanted from your life. And the poet replies that he has. When asked what it was that he wanted, he says, 'To call myself beloved.'

Jerry said that she cried when she read those lines. I asked why.

'You see, Susie, the truth is that I have been beloved in my marriage. I know what it is to be loved like that. The difficulty in very long marriages is not to lose it, and if one does, to find it again. To be beloved unconditionally over a very long time within a marital framework—is it possible? Was it ever possible? It's this possibility that has me in there ... still negotiating.'

Ann Hollingworth

Reading an article about how the Archbishop of Brisbane, Peter Hollingworth, had talked Opposition leader John Hewson into exempting food from the goods and services tax he was proposing before the March 1993 federal election, I began to wonder what his wife was like. No-one seemed to know anything about her. When I finally tracked down Peter's secretary and made my request to interview Ann, I did not expect the answer to be yes. Invisible wives of public figures usually prefer to stay that way.

I eventually came face to face with Ann Hollingworth in Melbourne, where she and Peter were staying at a friend's house. She said she was surprised that I wanted to talk to her. Her manner was friendly but guarded—very guarded. I was not sure whether this was Ann's real personality or whether I had simply failed to get beyond her role as the archbishop's wife. I left the interview feeling very unsatisfied.

Luckily, something went wrong with the original transcription and the first interview was wiped. The second interview took place on Ann's own turf, in the archbishop's grand residence in Brisbane. This time I felt she was a little more relaxed.

I'VE never seen myself as someone who challenges or rocks the boat. I usually try to keep things on an even keel and calm everyone down. But on occasions when I have been ignored and made to feel invisible, I have seethed away to myself and only expressed my anger to Peter on the way home in the car.

I know that Peter is there to take the service, so he is the prime reason everyone is there, but I think they should say, 'It's very nice to have the archbishop here this morning and Ann is here too.' A lot do say that, but on occasions I have been quite devastated.

Very often people don't see the archbishop's wife as an equal partner. I see myself as an equal partner. I realise that Peter has skills in the church that I don't have. Taking a service is part of his skill and part of his training; it's not part of mine.

I was born in 1936, the eldest of four girls, and we grew up in Melbourne. I went to an Anglican girls' school called Korowa in Glen Iris. My father was in business, my mother was educated as a teacher. Korowa was the sort of school that suited me. It gave me great opportunities to participate in a lot of things ranging from sport to the choir.

I didn't get into trouble—I wasn't a rebel. I was the sort of person who put a lot of effort into everything that I did. I took everything very seriously, was very conscientious and wanted to do well. Academically, I was about the middle of the class. I did much better at sport and discovered that what you do well, you put more energy into. I learned that what you put in, you get out, and I found this worked for me at school. At the end of the war we didn't have many social outlets, compared to the kids of today, so school was your whole life.

My mother stayed at home until I was fifteen, when she decided to go back to work, which was quite unusual in those days. She was a domestic science teacher. I must say it was a bit of a shock to us. I think she suddenly realised that she had a profession that she could financially make use of, so she decided to do it. She worked right up until retirement. We never really knew her age. I still don't know whether she was sixty or sixty-five when she retired.

I was elected vice-captain of the school, and house captain. When I was first elected house captain, I was really surprised. I thought, 'Why should they pick me?' But once I achieved that, I thought of myself as a leader and then it just seemed to happen—whenever I participated I always got into a team. I remember a friend saying, 'It's not fair. You go down there to get in, you always get in. I go down and never get in.' I realised then that if you participate and show you're enthusiastic you're more likely to do well.

At first I wanted to do medicine. My parents always had the idea that tertiary education was something you did; all my cousins had been tertiary educated. One did medicine and another did science, and so that was just the accepted thing, but when I went to the university I decided to do physiotherapy. I thought it would be less arduous than being a doctor and my mother very definitely encouraged me in that. They were good years, when I made lots of friends. Peter was at Trinity College; we were both at university together.

I met him at a dance when I was seventeen. Church dances were the equivalent of the discos today. I saw him and his friend on the bus. I was with a friend and we wondered where they were going. We talked about where *we* were going and of course they ended up at the same dance at St Oswald's in Glen Iris.

We danced all night—every second dance. Physically he was tall with a twinkle in his eye. Something clicked and I thought he was terrific. It was strange, because all my boyfriends had been little guys and suddenly along came this big guy. I had always had an image of myself with a tall man.

Peter was doing his National Service training in the Air Force at Point Cook, so he wasn't around a lot. But the next day he went around to a friend of his and said, 'I've met this girl and I don't know where she lives!' I was waiting for the phone to ring and hoping. I was very happy to be followed up. I was smitten. I was always smitten, but this time it seemed very different. Mind you, I wouldn't have liked my daughters to do the same thing at such a young age.

Peter decided to go into the ministry, which meant going back to school, doing matriculation, getting a Commonwealth Scholarship, and then going on to Trinity College at Melbourne University.

Being educated at an Anglican school, religion was incorporated into the whole curriculum, but I'd never, ever thought that I would marry a clergyman. I had been very influenced by Canon Bryan Green and his Mission at St Paul's Cathedral, but so had all the girls at school who had been to his rally. I had always done well in divinity, but it never occurred to me that this would be my life. When Peter announced that this was what he was going to do, I was quite shocked. I thought, 'Goodness me!', but I didn't really take in the implications.

We didn't speak about marriage right away, but I thought this would be the person I would marry. When we had been going out for a few months, we discussed whether we should go out with other people—but we decided we didn't really want to. I have no idea if he ever actually proposed to me.

Going into the ministry meant Peter would do three years of an arts degree, two years of a theological degree. In those days the church didn't like their curates to be married, so we could see seven years down the track.

I just accepted it. In those days people were getting married younger, but I was going to university and had my physio course, which was three years. Then I wanted to work a bit and could see five years, anyway, for establishing my own career. I would love to have got married right there and then, but from a practical perspective it wasn't possible.

At the age of seventeen I'd had a few boyfriends—and been in love with some of them. I enjoyed school dances and having lots of boyfriends. It seems horrific now to make that commitment so young. As you get older it is harder to make decisions—you become fussy.

I had never met anybody like Peter who was so concerned about the rest of the world. My life had been very sheltered, in a middle-class house, going to a middle-class school. He certainly opened my eyes to what was happening to people who didn't have as much as us. As a child his great hero was Robin Hood. He thinks differently now, but this was how it started. It was all a great surprise to me I was trying to take it all in but I was also battling with my own background.

Initially, we didn't have much discussion about it. He mostly talked and I listened. It didn't really hit me until we were first married and lived in the vicarage in North Melbourne and then I actually saw what he was talking about—the deserted wives, the children who didn't have fathers, the poverty, the people without jobs. I had never known anyone without a job. Unemployment wasn't something that had come across my horizons and if it had I hadn't thought too much about it.

When I saw it all first-hand, I became convinced that what

Peter said was right. Living in that part of Melbourne was very good for both of us. If he had gone to a middle-class parish, like St Andrew's, Brighton, which was the plum place to go as a curate, things could have been very different. These things don't happen by accident. Archdeacon Sambell, who later became Archbishop of Perth, chose Peter to go to North Melbourne because he knew what sort of person was wanted in that particular situation, having started out there himself. That really was the beginning of our married life; after that Peter went on to the Brotherhood of St Laurence and became the chaplain, and for the next twenty-five years this was his primary work, although he was still involved in the church.

I graduated, and then a year later we were married. I was twenty-four. I had started a new career and that was good fun.

I thought marriage was going to be lovely. I had a totally idealistic approach. I knew it wasn't going to be quite the same life as my friends were leading, in that once they were married they had a lot of time to themselves. But when the reality of our life hit me, I was shocked. I suddenly realised this was going to be no ordinary marriage. There weren't going to be nights at home cuddled up by the fire. There would be no great social life. I had a husband who disappeared into his study every night to write the next sermon, or who was always out at meetings. We were very fortunate because next door to us were a couple of social workers; the chap worked for the Brotherhood. We became a little community, and I think that was my salvation. They were tremendously supportive to both Peter and me. Peter had very high ideals, and when he discovered all the middle-class skills he had didn't work in a low socio-economic parish he was pretty desperate. Having social workers next door really did help him to see what was happening.

I was working at Mount Royal Geriatric Hospital, which was close by, and I loved it. I suddenly saw that there was a tremendous amount to working with old people, particularly the importance of humour. In those days anybody who was ill and old was kept in bed; today the elderly are properly dressed and treated as people. I enjoyed the challenge of working with people recovering from strokes, helping to get them on their feet again. We also had a 'relatives day' when the rellies came

in and we showed them what was going on and how to help them when they went home. It was imperative that they could be independent and maximise the amount of physical ability they had, even with the effects of a disability.

I worked from nine till five and Peter and I would always have our evening meal together. He'd help me with the dinner and then he'd go out to a meeting. I was grumpy about him going to so many meetings. I don't know how we survived those first six months. I thought marriage wasn't much chop and a great disappointment, but I felt I had made my bed and had to lie in it.

My attitude changed a bit when I realised we were meeting

a lot of interesting people. That has been the pattern of our lives; it hasn't changed. Over the years there have always been meetings, and I saw them as more of a threat to marriage and family life as the years went by, but I didn't actually complain in the beginning. I realised it was a very hard parish, with a lot of social problems, and could see the enormity of the work. I accepted that. It just had to be done.

I used to go to the flat next door for meals, and we've done that all through the years, or people have dropped in on us. We have always had lots of friends around us and I've gained a great deal of support from them. As the years go by you make friends together. I'm still very close to a lot of my physio friends and my school friends, but you pick up more as you go and that's how I managed to cope with an absentee husband.

I accepted that that was the life of a young curate, but as the years went by I began to challenge those ideas. When we had children I realised he wasn't seeing much of them. Just as he challenges people, he is very easily challenged too. And if I said, 'You haven't seen the kids' or 'These are the children's activities—could you plan your commitments accordingly?' he would. It was a good family life in that respect, although it did have to be worked at. When I deliberately decided that was the way it had to be, it worked well.

Peter was never ambitious for himself. There has always been a job to do, issues to follow, but it was never a personal ambition. In a way that is almost harder. If you can see somebody working for themselves and for their family you think, 'Oh well, there's a spin-off'. But he was always working for other people and for justice issues.

Our first daughter was born two years after we married. At first I was very frightened of having children, but then suddenly I got that marvellous maternal instinct and was thrilled at being pregnant.

Peter didn't see the birth. We got to the hospital and everything was happening so quickly that I was rushed into the delivery room. He would have been there but the doctor arrived. I can remember saying to the doctor, 'Peter's outside,' and he said, 'Well, bring him in,' so he held her as I held her. He was present for all the other births. As a physio his being there was something very important to me, especially as I was teaching fathers to be involved in the delivery. With the second pregnancy he went along to some fathers' classes and it was a very positive experience for both of us. Being home during the day, he had a lot of involvement with the baby. One of the spin-offs of being in a parish is that the fathers are around during the day, if not at night.

When the second baby came along, I was doing a lot of private work at home and I really felt I was in the workforce. It helped because it helped keep my identity as a person. I viewed it as a really exciting experience, being a physiotherapist. Working with pregnancy parents then became the focus of my physiotherapy life. I began by having a few patients, and that eventually developed into quite a good private practice. Having a bit of work gave me something else to think about and financially I suddenly had a little bit of money of my own. If I left Peter to pay bills they'd never be paid, so I was always the one who looked after those things. He never thinks about money—it's there and that's all.

I don't organise his day. That's done by other people. Somebody has to keep the home fires burning, rolling along and organised. It's very easy for things to get disorganised in the sort of life we lead. I do make an attempt to make sure things are in order.

Peter has always gone out of his way to support me in my profession and did anything he could do to help me. As a person working with expectant parents I used to work at night, too, so if he could baby-sit he would, and he would prepare the meal.

We like to have people around us, and do lots of things. You know how some husbands are grumpy if there's a party on or, if they've been invited to dinner, they say they're too tired? Peter will always join in. If I say 'I really would like to do this,' he won't say no. He'll always meet me halfway and discuss it. But as for running in with breakfast on a tray every morning, forget it. I get a cup of tea occasionally.

I'm the one who does the cooking. He's okay for a scrambled egg—he could survive, but he's not one of these New Age men who like the kitchen and will come in and make something fantastic. He'd help clean up and take out the rubbish. He enjoys the garden and doing things around the house, but there's little time.

We discuss everything and are very open with one another, and we have had some good arguments. They're usually over very mundane things, something that is niggling at the back of your mind. Maybe we'd had a rotten week when he wasn't home much and the kids were getting me down. We'd have a vigorous debate and then it's all over. No sulking. Probably a big hug and a cuddle.

We were always a physical couple and that's a nice part of marriage. Peter is a person who likes to show affection. He's a 'man's man', but he also enjoys the company of women. There have always been women who have found him very attractive and loved talking to him at a party. Initially I used to be jealous and would tell him. Now I would go off in the opposite direction and find somebody to have a little flirt with myself.

We can both enjoy people of the opposite sex, but we both trust each other because our marriage is secure and strong. When you're a clergyman or priest people might flirt with you, but fidelity is a vital part of a Christian marriage. My marriage and Peter are so important to me I make every effort to work any problem through, and so does he.

I don't think he could manage without me. He always says I'm his anchor. I'm really a little terrier that chomps away at his ankles and doesn't let him go. They all say I'm very small but very bossy.

I think it's an equal relationship now, but it hasn't always been totally equal. The women's movement has rubbed off on everybody a bit. I was never a member, although I thought it very important. I'm very committed to the idea of women having equal rights and equal roles in life and working for their independence, but I always see things as a partnership, too. My aim is that we would have an equal partnership. I recognise that Peter's job in life is difficult and that he needs a lot of support. You can't have two stars in one family. I was very happy to be a mother and a part-time physio; it actually suited

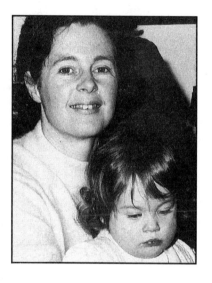

me very well. Peter always enjoyed the fact that I was a physiotherapist. People would come up to him at parties and say, 'You're Ann Hollingworth's husband; my wife came to her for our baby' or 'I actually came to your house and I sat on your floor as a father and was involved in the classes.' He took a delight in that part of our partnership.

Peter shares those things that he is able to share. For him, home is where you can come and unwind. He loves talking, not only to me, but to everybody. I'll always put my two-penny-worth in. Sometimes he holds the floor, and it's very hard to get a word in edgeways, but I always will if I really want to. He is aware that he has a stronger voice and is more influential, but he doesn't speak over me. He always tries to involve me in the conversation, too.

In the early days he would hold the floor at dinner parties and I would get into him afterwards, 'You held the floor for too long. It really was a bit much. It was good fun until you got onto your strong issues.' These days I don't have to say anything because he's taken what I think on board.

My daughters think I'm tough on him. Once he bought six punnets of strawberries for a dollar instead of buying good strawberries for twice the price. I said, 'Peter, you're so stupid!' and my daughters said, 'Oh, Mum, at least he went out and bought the strawberries.' But they think it's quite funny when I get stuck into him. They know we're very close.

Peter has these flights of fancy, these visions, and I'm often the one to say, 'Come off it, that won't work.' But if he still went ahead, then that would be his decision; I wouldn't influence him to change track. He is a professional person who thinks through what he's doing. I respect his decisions and his intellectual ability.

I'm not really aware of people trying to influence Peter through me. Many years ago a doctor talked to me about abortion and I was quite sure he was intending it to get through to Peter, but I made it quite clear to that doctor that there was no way that what he said would be passed on to Peter.

In the past people have pushed past me to get to Peter, and that has irritated me. Now I know how to cope with it. I walk off in the other direction and go and talk to somebody else. It's stupid behaviour because afterwards I usually tell Peter what I think of such people.

I think Peter looks very handsome when he's all done up in his clerical regalia. I admire the physical. A lot of church leaders have an enormous array of copes and mitres, but Peter only has a few. It has all been part of our lives now for such a long time that it's not something I think about. But it never occurred to me that I would be married to an archbishop. I always think of him as my husband first. I couldn't imagine life without him, apart from death. It has always been like that. I think I'm extremely lucky, even though he's sometimes a handful.

The hardest time for me has been coming to Brisbane, losing my job, my family, my home; it was very difficult. Also a very close friend who had been a patient of mine died. That happened in May and I moved here in June, and I felt I had lost everything. Peter was having extreme problems with moving into a new job with no resources. I've never felt so depressed and sad. I think I really lost my identity; I didn't know who I was. Four years down the track I feel like me again, but at that stage, rattling around in this big house, with no children, no job and strangers everywhere was ghastly. Every Sunday we would go to a parish and get lost because we didn't know the city. I don't think I ever thought of leaving, but I used to wake up in the morning crying, and go to bed crying. It upset him enormously because there was nothing he could do about it.

I kept thinking it was like the first six months of our marriage, when I used to think, 'I just have to hang on—it will get better.' And it has got better. You come in as an archbishop and wife and people expect you to behave in those roles, but then you've got to be accepted as yourselves. It's very difficult for people to look at an archbishop as a person, a neighbour and a friend. We had it all in Melbourne; we never really had to work at any of those things. Suddenly I had to work at relationships, work at making friends, work at managing a house, work at finding a new identity. I have never felt more lost and lonely. Peter was at the peak of his career and I was miserable and desperate. I should have gone and got professional help, but I didn't. I was listening to somebody talking about helping politicians come through post-election syndrome when they lose their seats, and I felt I was definitely suffering a similar sort of grief and depression. Somehow I managed to work through it myself. I used to ring up my friends in Melbourne, but I don't ring them nearly as much now.

We have three daughters. Deborah, the eldest is a lawyer, and she is an issues person like her father. Our second daughter, Fiona, is a Bachelor of Education and is looking for a job. Sarah, our third, is at Melbourne University and working part-time. Though each of them is different, they are all very aware of social issues, having lived in a household like ours and having grown up in Fitzroy.

The first time we went overseas we were very fortunate in that a parishioner paid for Peter to go on a study tour. He felt it was extremely important that I went too, so we took the children and were away six months. The other occasions Peter went overseas I didn't go. I had a career which I just couldn't drop. Nevertheless if Peter is invited to a conference as guest speaker they don't automatically say they'd like me to come too. If I desperately wanted to go I probably would, but I would have to find the money. It's a bonus when provision is made for me.

There are a lot of very positive things about being married to a public person. Doors open to a lot of interesting experiences, like Peter being Australian of the Year—that was a very positive experience for us both. You have to line everything up, the good with the bad.

When Peter was at the Brotherhood, I didn't necessarily go to all the things he went to because of the children. But once they were older and he became a bishop we did a lot more together.

When he was offered Brisbane, I had a marvellous job as a physio in a private orthopaedic unit. I'd been there for fifteen months and the staff said jokingly 'Do you have to go? Couldn't you commute?' But I don't think it would have been very good for us as a couple. If I had to toss up between my marriage and my job, I'd go for my marriage every time.

Peter felt a very strong calling to come to Brisbane, and there's no way I would not have come. These days, though, when clergymen are asked to go to a particular place, they often refuse because it will upset the children's schooling or their wife's got a job. Often the wives' jobs are better paid than the husband's. Peter had been at the Brotherhood of St Laurence for twenty-five years and I had a sense that something else would happen.

If Peter died, I would have to move. I would have to find myself a house, and pick up a career again. I'm still doing a bit of physio, and attend seminars and workshops to keep the academic side of things going. If I had to pick it up again I could. Obviously there would be people who would cut you off the invitation list, and that would probably be hurtful. I've heard of that happening, but I could cope with it. I would probably go back to Melbourne, where the children are, pick up my life and my friends. I hope to God it doesn't happen; I would be personally devastated. But I would take it on as a challenge and I would survive.

In the church, you don't have to inherit the previous arch-bishop's wife's role. I do what I think needs to be done and nobody has ever questioned that. If I go back to work, that's fine. But it's tricky, because we have a very busy life. Yet we both think it's important that I make some life of my own, a separate life. I try and play tennis with friends. There are a lot of functions to attend and I have to toss up. Peter might go by himself, but that's pretty lonely when you're in a new place, and if you don't go to things you never get to know people, or I try to go with him as much as possible. Peter is number one ticket-holder for the Brisbane Bears and I went with him to the opening of the social club. I didn't have to go, but I went be-cause going out and meeting people increases your knowledge of the place, and the more people you meet the easier it is. I like to get out and about and to be involved.

But basically I run Bishopsbourne. I do have some help, but resources are limited. In the church you do get 'two for the price of one'. I suppose I could kick up a fuss about it, but I wouldn't. If we are having a function then I try to get some help, but I do a lot myself and I think most archbishops' wives do the same around the country. Some women are very happy to help and do it by choice. There's a certain amount of my life where I choose to help Peter because the church's re-sources are so limited. I see that as part of my commitment as a Christian. At the same time I realise that it's very important to have an identity of my own and try to have some sort of separate life, too. I'm determined to achieve it.

Ann was more reticent during her interviews than the other women had been. When I left—and even afterwards—she was concerned that she had revealed too much. I assured her that compared to the candour of some of the other women, she had been cautious indeed! It was clear that even though her husband feels free to speak out on a range of issues, Ann felt the need to be guarded: perhaps it goes with the territory.

Celebrating the Self

Patrice Newell

Rosemary Tipiloura

Cherryl Barassi

Part III   Celebrating the Self

These three women, Patrice Newell, Rosemary Tipiloura and Cherryl Barassi, had an early sense of themselves as individuals with the right to choose. They had a highly developed sense of self-worth, which meant that when they met their partners it was a case of 'This is me. Take me on my own terms or forget it.' They all lead two lives, their own and the one they share with their partners. Neither life is more important than the other. They began their relationships on the basis of equal partnerships and have never compromised that equality.

None was brought up in a traditional family. Patrice was an only child with both parents at work, Rosemary grew up in Aboriginal culture and Cherryl had a totally eccentric, peripatetic childhood. These women had an early awareness of choice, of their lives being something that they would create for themselves. They were never impressed by wealth or status or class, and never pursued these options.

Their own sense of space is very important to them. They don't expect a man to be all things to them or the partnership to fulfil all their needs.

Patrice does not insist that Phillip knows how to run the farm, or feel that she has to listen to his radio program. Cherryl doesn't want to know about football, and doesn't expect Ron to share her passion for art. Rosemary doesn't want to know about politics or expect Bob to take on her cultural beliefs.

They respect their partners, they believe in their talents and share their values. They never inhibit each other's freedom or try to change the other's behaviour. They are realists who like to get on with life and with their own interests. They are great survivors, because each has a strong bedrock of self-esteem and a clear sense of personal direction. They are able to integrate their public lives with their private passions because they celebrate their own sense of self and know its value.

Patrice Newell

Phillip Adams's producer told me that Patrice Newell did not talk about her life with Phillip—in fact, she has never talked to the media about anything since she left television. When I tracked Patrice down by phone she was very wary. 'I said when I left "The Today Show" that I'd never give another interview.'

'Why?'

'Because it's all just so many lies.'

'But what about one that tells the truth?'

'All that media hype and celebrity stuff is nothing compared to the richness and satisfaction of my life in the country.'

'Well, this is the chance to say that.'

'Look, we're about to go overseas. I couldn't possibly think about it at the moment.'

'What if I ring when you get back? Think about it while you're away.'

When I rang back a few months later and explained the kind of interviews I had already done for the book and what I was trying to achieve, she agreed to meet me in their house in Sydney.

Dressed in jeans and a shirt, no make-up, perfect complexion, the teeth that made Macleans toothpaste a household name—I could hardly recognise Patrice as the person I had last seen on morning television.

Having decided to talk to me, she was straightforward and forthright in her opinions. The conversation was easy and unself-conscious.

THE media always describe you by the last thing you did. So they say of me, 'She used to be on "The Today Show".' All through my twenties when I was doing current affairs or reading the news on TV, people would say to me, 'Weren't you the Macleans girl?' Other people hang onto your past as if the past is the only relevant thing.

I was born in 1956. I remember Vatican II and am exactly the same age as the girls in 'Brides of Christ'. I lived in Kurralta Park in Adelaide and went to a working-class Catholic primary school, St Joseph's, and then to St Aloysius in the city. St Aloysius was a very good radical school. Most of the nuns that taught me have left. A whole group of them were having affairs with the local Christian Brothers down the road. This was the Sixties and Seventies. All my best friends are Catholic; I still have an innate affinity with Catholic girls. I was actually a very conscientious student, but not a very good one.

I was an only child and greatly loved. My father worked in hotels behind the bar and then he went on to work for the General Post Office and most of the time my mother worked at Hush Puppies making shoes on the assembly line. It was a classic case of parents coming home physically worn out and deafened by the sound of the workplace. It was a secure and safe childhood. It was not a jolly, joyous household; they were busy enough not to indulge me.

I don't know what they wanted for me. When you are growing up in the western suburbs in any city you know that your parents don't have the same ambition that parents in the eastern suburbs have. They don't perceive their children's futures in the same way. I started modelling in Adelaide when I was thirteen or fourteen.

I had actually thought about university but it was unaffordable. I did end up going to university later. I did not pass matric the first time because I had glandular fever in the third term. I did all right the second time, but I never did well in exams. I left school thinking I just had to get on with it. I decided to be a nurse.

I was booked in to do my nursing training at Darwin hospital when the cyclone hit. They would not take trainees, but notified me to hang about. I went up there to check it out, but with so many men there it was not a good place for a young girl straight out of school. I decided I didn't like it and in the meantime had started modelling, earning good money, and ended up coming to Sydney. I gave nursing a miss and got an agent. Basically I was just your classic scrubber trying to make a quid, carrying a portfolio.

I was only eighteen. I could not wait to get out of Adelaide. I looked at the map and decided I did not want my future to be there. I desperately wanted to get out. I had been to Sydney during school holidays when I was sixteen, and thought Sydney was very glamorous. I still think it is.

The shift in energy level from Adelaide to Sydney was huge; it was like when I first went to New York and there was another huge leap. You just can't help being invigorated by it. I felt a great need to spend some time there and let it rub off and I did live in New York for a year and a half.

When I was in my twenties, I was an all right model. I made an average living out of it, but never a huge amount of money. While I was modelling I decided to do arts at the University of New South Wales.

During the holidays my boyfriend Cameron Allen and I bought some cheap tickets to the US. I took my portfolio with me. I got an agent to take me on in New York and when I went back to university in Sydney I thought, 'What am I doing here?' I decided to leave, earn a lot of money and move back to New York.

My modelling career never took off, but it was just such a wonderful experience to actually live there. I left New York and lived in Chicago, where I did quite well. Cameron and I married at Niagara Falls in 1980. Then I stayed on in Chicago and Cameron returned to Sydney. Cameron's father became very sick and was in intensive care, so I came home. I commuted between Chicago and Sydney for a while but eventually the more I stayed in Sydney the more my attitude to modelling changed. I am a fairly serious person and I think one of the reasons why I didn't always do well was that I was always trying to talk to people, whereas all they wanted to know was whether my bust was thirty-five and my waist twenty-five. Once I stopped caring about it, I seemed to get all the jobs so I went back to Chicago, packed up and came back to Sydney.

I decided I had to get out of modelling, but I didn't quite know how I was going to do it. In New York everyone you met seemed to be a writer, actor, dancer or budding film director, so I was encouraged to start writing. I did some journalism in Chicago and had a few things published. When I came home I did a bit of freelance work. I have always lived on small amounts of money, mostly because I'm incredibly tight.

One of my great attributes was that I never spent money on clothes. Kids today seem to spend 50 per cent of their income on clothing, but I never did. I was never interested in clothes. Modelling was good in that it provided me with the means of moving to Sydney, and living and working in America. But I was always a realist. From an early age I never ever confused the image that you project in a magazine or television with who I was as a person.

I had absorbed a lot of feminist thought. I was fourteen when Germaine Greer came on the scene and the abortion issue came up. That was a pretty big deal, being Catholic. It was such a hot issue that teachers left school over it.

My mother was a fairly tough, independent, energetic person. Circumstances led to her working in a factory. She was a very smart working-class woman, and a good role model.

When I came to Sydney, one of the first people I met when I was learning Japanese at night school was a woman who went on to become the secretary of WEL. I went along to assertiveness training meetings. All that sitting around seems funny now, but I was glad I was part of it.

I often wonder what they thought about me. Now when I see Eva Cox and all those great women, even though our lives were so different I feel a great sense of pride that I was involved in that early stuff. When I was modelling I used to go to the WEL office and hang around. They'd be typing newsletters and organising protests. I loved the atmosphere and the discussion.

I wasn't concerned with finding Mr Right; I looked at it more in terms of choosing to have a life alone or having a shared life. I think being an only child you do grow up fairly self-sufficient and it is easy to just be by yourself. When I came to Sydney and didn't know anybody I could easily fill an empty Sunday, just walking in the streets and the parks, and catching buses. Being alone was never a big thing for me even in New York. If I have an afternoon free it never occurs to me to feel lonely; I can just read a book.

It was not so much that I had to have a man; it was just that the whole world was out there and I did not want to sit around and waste time. But I didn't think I needed a man to have an exciting life.

I sometimes feel like I've had only had two relationships in my life. I had casual boyfriends, but met Cameron when I was twenty. Everyone thinks they have high standards. If you don't get attention from anyone else in your life then it's different. When you are a model you have all these people fussing over you. When you go home the last thing you want is to be fussed over. It is the same if you work in TV. Everybody thinks I did this huge leap from being a model to being a journalist on TV, but you know, if you are really honest it is not such a huge leap. I'm not saying it is a natural extension, but the journalism part is pretty small when you are on TV. No matter how much all the female journalists on TV like to make out that appearance does not matter, it is just nonsense. It still matters a lot.

It's totally different for men on television. It is impossible to imagine a female version of Laurie Oakes on TV.

So there I was in my early twenties, thinking, 'I have to get out of this modelling stuff one day, but how am I going to do it?' There were quite a lot of people doing freelance writing and succeeding. It appeared to me at the time that if I could write one really great story, that would be a turning point. Most of my friends had written something that had then caught someone's eye and given them a real start.

My big break, when it came, was a flukey bit of good luck. Anna Maria Monticelli was a model and her husband Rick Jemison was the assistant news director at Channel Seven. We were sitting around one night and she said, 'Why don't you go out and have a word with Rick?' So I talked to Rick and subsequently he showed me around the newsroom. He told me to read Tom Wolfe and get into New Journalism. I did as I was told.

He rang me back about six months later. I'll always remember the phone call because he rang up late at night and said, 'Do you still want to be a serious person, Patrice?' and I said, 'Yes, yes, yes!' and he hired me to be a researcher for Kerry O'Brien on the documentary he was doing called 'Circle of Poison'. That was my break into journalism, and a real turning point in my life.

The documentary triggered my interest in pesticide residues in agriculture. If it had not been for finding out about chemicals through that work I probably would not have become seriously interested in farming or be doing what I am doing now. Kerry was great; tough and demanding. Then we did a project on unemployment together. It was mainly desk work, but I loved it.

My last modelling job was a cover for *Family Circle*. Cameron was absolutely happy for me to get a new job, but he was never keen on journalism. He pushed this line, which I have only begun to appreciate and share now, which is that the precarious nature of journalism is essentially the underlying unsatisfying aspect of it. Journalists are mostly unsatisfied people and I think that is because, if you are only ever snooping around other people's lives, that energy is not really going into building your own life. It ended up like that for me, and a lot of other people, I'm sure. Cameron always thought if I was going to write I should be concentrating on fiction. Something dramatic, something which had more resonance.

At the time I was just so incredibly pleased, firstly to have a job and secondly to get out of modelling. And to work with someone like Kerry was really falling on your feet. When Kerry became an American correspondent for Channel Seven, I did the overnight news shift at Seven.

I did not think I was dumb, but I did not think I was really bright; there is a difference. I didn't think I always dealt with intellectually demanding situations very well. But I wanted to. I had found university one of the most disappointing experiences. I was originally there for the eighteen months but then I went back again part-time when I was at SBS. You expect your tutorials to have a dynamic about them, but they didn't.

When I was at Channel 7, Vincent Smith, who has since passed away, was the news director and he sent me off to voice lessons with Max Rowley, who also gave me some training in reading the news. After the evening bulletin I would be allowed to sit in a chair and read the autocue, which irritated the life out the crew, who had to stay back a few extra minutes. They gave me the video tape so that I could look back on it and see what I was doing. There was never any suggestion of job offers; it was just some sort of training to see if I had any potential. After a year when it became pretty clear that I was never going to get out of the overnight shift at Channel 7, that I was doomed to be there what felt like forever, I put together a tape and sent it over to SBS. I knew there was a vacancy and I got the job. So I worked on the news desk for three days at SBS and read the news at the weekend. SBS had a fantastic team of people. I stayed for nearly three years.

There was a big fight going on at SBS between two people; a whole bunch of us backed the one who lost and my life was doomed. At that stage I was presenting a current affairs show called 'Midweek', which had been going about nine months. I knew he was going to axe it and that basically he did not like me, so my days were probably numbered. That's how you live on television, with an axe permanently poised above your head.

At that stage I was thinking not so much of leaving Cameron as getting another place. He wrote his music from home and I thought it was pretty important to have my own place. In fact I became quite obsessed with it.

I had some employment options and I chose the one with the most money. That was probably an insane decision, and it might not have been a wild success story career-wise, but it enabled me to buy my own place and have it paid off within a year. That was 'The Today Show', but I must say I hadn't planned on leaving when I did.

I never liked the show. It was mostly boring. I never even watched it. Channel 9 had rung me putting feelers out, so I felt that if I wanted the job, I could get it. In the industry it is regarded as a pretty good job. Steve Leibmann was already there. I talked to Peter Hanrahan, the former news director at SBS, about it. He said, 'You could do it.' I thought that I could just 'do it' like I 'did' modelling, but you really need to believe that what you are doing is important to do it well. I mean, you don't write even your own questions on 'The Today Show'. You just read the briefs and all the questions are written for you. You only have to read the autocue.

I had to do a few 'celebrity' things and make myself available. I quite liked doing it at SBS, because it needed all the publicity it could get, but by the time I got to Channel 9 I had said everything there was to say anyway. It was more about having a certain image portrayed of you. Let's face it, anyone who believes that trash in any of those magazines is just pathetically stupid. It's very easy for people to lie in interviews.

The past really is a foreign country, because you look back on it and you try and work out why you did things. Sometimes it is painful to deal with decisions you made that you think are not so honourable.

Now that I am dealing with people at the farm, where I am the employer, I think greatly about the responsibility of the employer. It's easy when you are only an employee; you try and get as much as you possibly can out of the system. As an employer I have found I have been assessing my motives a lot more. I think probably it would have been better if I had never taken the 'Today' job. There were a couple of other jobs going that were much better, but they paid one-third of the money—I was only thinking of the money. It was a big thing to be able to totally pay off a house in Sydney.

During the course of that year on 'The Today Show' I left my husband. Phillip and I had met the year before when I interviewed him for SBS, and he came to Sydney to live a few months later. He had been in Melbourne, and married, and I look back on it now and I think our coming together was inevitable, but at the time it wasn't. He bought a house in Darlinghurst, and I had moved into a flat. At the same time my father in Adelaide had been told he had terminal cancer. Phillip was the perfect person to be around when dealing with the death of someone close to you. Although death had been something I had thought about superficially, being with Phillip was a very confronting thing. All at once, I had the demands of the job, plus dealing with the sadness of leaving Cameron, trying to get it together with Phillip, and Dad dying in Adelaide.

It was about six months before he finally died. I would leave 'The Today Show' at nine a.m. on Friday, walk off the set and Phillip would be there to pick me up. We would drive across to Adelaide, choosing a different route every time. It was a great opportunity to spend a lot of time talking. We would spend a night in a motel, the next night in Adelaide, the next night in a motel and I would be back on the set to start at four-thirty a.m. Monday. We did that for many, many weeks and it was a very consolidating time for Phillip and me. We also got to see a lot of Australia and started thinking about buying a place together. We had a fantasy about a place in the country, a little house in a pretty valley. It started off as a weekender and then gradually we looked around and our ambitions got bigger and bigger until we ended up buying 7000 acres at Scone.

Dad died in the October and I got fired in the November, and then we went overseas for eight weeks. We did this big European jaunt that we had been planning. We went to Egypt, Europe and America in December and January. It was time to have an adventure, and by the time we returned to Australia the papers for the farm had been done. We moved into the farm and I took on the running of it.

I don't really want to talk about why I was fired, because I can't really tell you the truth. It involves some pretty mean things about a few of the people. Basically they weren't happy with me and were much happier with Liz Hayes for a whole lot of other reasons.

I always get a bit melodramatic about getting fired, but I had an opportunity to stay on there. It wasn't like, 'Get out of here! We never want to see you again!' One of the options was being an arts reporter and there was an offer of a current affairs show in Melbourne. If I had wanted to stay in television, I probably would have accepted one of those jobs, but by the time I had got to 'The Today Show' I was already thinking about leaving television. I knew I was not going to spend the rest of my life doing this. It's nice to have your ego massaged and politicians duchessing you, but you know why they're doing it. And if you don't you are in real trouble.

Sometimes I think people don't want to give up those jobs

because they don't want to be crossed off the invitation list.

I must say it did not feel good to get fired, just the same. Phillip says I handled it well, but the day it happened I was really angry about the way it was done. I would have preferred Sam Chisholm to have been honest. Our last half-a-dozen conversations were just bullshit, and I thought, 'This is pathetic, that it has come to this.' That's what you have to put up with. In TV when you are a bit on the outer or on the nose, people rub it in and are quite mean to you. There's an expression, 'Schadenfreude', where basically all your friends really like the fact that you are about to get the flick or be shafted or the boss has said something mean about you. They really secretly enjoy it. There is so much of that in television. It confirmed all my feelings about what television was really like.

So I went from that world to the farm. Phillip and I were really babes in the wood. We often wonder if, if we had known what we were getting into, whether we'd have ever done it. The answer is probably no. The temperament required for rural life is of a particular kind, and initially I wondered whether I had it.

Now I move to the beat of a different drum, but I don't feel intellectually any slower. Originally when we bought it we thought Phillip would come up, and then circumstances did not really allow that to happen. Now we have a good routine going where we both basically work like crazy and then Phillip comes up and the four days we are together are great. We are both very good at organising time. One of our great strengths is that we have certainly got our priorities right in that department.

Now that our baby Rory—Aurora—is around, a lot more time is dedicated to her, but even so, there are certain parts of the day when I deliberately don't take her with me. I get up at six a.m. and do the usual chores after feeding her and me, then

she has a little sleep and I usually do an hour of bookwork. I
sometimes see Phil Gilbert, my right-hand man. He comes in
usually at eight, or we talk on the phone. He might be out
mustering the cattle in the yards and he will ring me and say,

'I will meet you at the yards at one. Don't forget the vaccine.'
We go down and pick out heifers that look like they might get
eye cancer, then I go back and get the mail, go home, get
lunch. My mother lives in another house on the property so
sometimes I can leave Rory with her. There is a large garden,
pumps to check, troughs to check, cattle to check.

Gardening has become a complete obsession with me. I
don't do as much as I would like, but I think about it a lot. It's
gardening in the mind as much as gardening in the ground.
When we moved to the farm one of my ambitions was to plant
a truly great garden. I have looked at a lot of gardens around
the world and have had a lot of ideas on what I wanted to do,
but I've had to concentrate on other priorities.

We did not really allocate enough money for buying stock, which was quite good in a way because the stock gradually built up. There's a 700 breeding herd, so during spring we have 700 cows with 700 calves. It's a lot. We produce and market 'Elmswood Beef'. It is a bio-dynamic farm, so we don't use chemicals or superphosphate. It's just a question of managing those animals as best we can in the most healthy way, which has been a nightmare for the last two years of the drought. My job is to observe. I am out seeing if the grass is overgrazed, or deciding whether, having let that weed go to seed, we have to slash, or if the native trees are growing in this area, whether they are being damaged by too much stock. These questions totally absorb me. Farmers are self-taught. I talk a lot to the neighbours and the Department of Agriculture.

In the beginning we had two full-time men, and now we have one full-time man and one casual. It's a job demanding great organisation because a cattle property is about cattle management, pasture management and money management. It's three separate jobs, in a way, and I can't believe how fascinating I find it.

We are planning a big diversification, so I think we will be there for a while. In the back of my mind I always wanted to be rural. In fact, when I was with Cameron, I kept in the back of my wardrobe a box of old clothes and I always said, 'That's for when we have a farm.' Whether he threw them out—he was a great one for throwing things out—or whether he talked me into throwing them out I don't know, but they disappeared. And when they did it was like the dream went with them.

If we had just bought a house in the country it would be a very quiet life, but this is not a quiet life. Having a farm is a business. Your network is the stock and station agents, the Department of Agriculture, the Forestry Commission and all the other farmers. It's not like I am out there just sitting about at nights. I have a lot of bookwork to do.

If I had known being a mother was so good I would have done it ages ago. Lots of my friends had kids, and no-one actually told me how great it was. There is always this talk about, 'Oh, I never get any time' or 'I am always tired', but that's not been my experience. There are days certainly when she is more demanding, but I only find myself quite fatigued by it if it's been a really busy business day. If I have to carry her around I can say, 'Mum, can you look after her for ten minutes? I have to make this phone call. I forgot to ring and book a truck.' What no-one told me and I never expected is that Rory gives me energy. She gives me so much happiness, she enlightens me, and that's why I have not felt tired. There is never this feeling of being taken from, that I expected.

Phillip is a doting father. Right from the beginning he always did his share of looking after her. I'm not having any more children, but I don't think being an only child is a negative thing. Even though Phillip is seventeen years older than me, he is not like a portly cigar-smoking heavy drinker, eating-a-big-three-course-meal person. He is the most energetic, dynamic young person, much more energetic than any man I have ever met. We have been together eight years. I would rather have had the eight years with Phillip, even if he dropped dead tomorrow. I don't worry about the future; it would be awful if it happened, but I think it's highly unlikely.

He is a 'get on with it' person. He is the best person in the world to travel with; I just adore it. To travel with him is the ultimate joy, because he is interested in everything; nothing is ever boring. We have just come back from this epic trip where we travelled 8000 kilometres with Aurora. We drove to Italy across France to Spain and back again. From Rome to Florence, the pollution was so devastating you could hardly see fifty metres in front of the car. The big lie of travelling is that the real event is when you arrive. But the joy is not arriving at the other end; it is the journey along the way. I always believed that, but never shared it with anyone until I travelled with Phillip.

He really wanted to be the tour guide for my first trip to Egypt and if we never did any other travel that's what he wanted to do the most. I said, 'I am so glad I am going with you; I could have gone before, but how wonderful now that this is going to happen because I will get so much more out of it. You will know so much we won't have to look it up in books—you will just be able to tell me.' He said, 'And if I don't I will make it up.' Ever since then if ever he says anything with great authority I always think, 'Perhaps he is making it up,' which he would not, one hopes. But he can always string a good story together.

We talk every day on the phone. I don't listen to his radio program, but if he is really excited about an interview he'll ring me and we'll talk about it. Everything is interesting to him still; he is never bored. And neither am I. It's the diversity of my life that I love. When I drive around the farm I'm a lot more at ease than I used to be, but of course there is still tons to know. There is something intrinsic and innate about a lot of the cattlemen that I don't have and I really would love to have. I used to think I can go into a museum or an art gallery and walk around and feel very comfortable, having looked at millions of paintings around the world. I go out into a paddock and I look at a hundred head of Herefords and they still all look the same to me. Only now am I beginning to get that flavour of what's good and what's not good, what's working, what's not working. I am still confused with black cattle. The breeders walk in and they know all the different Angus because their noses are a bit different, but that's something you only get after a long involvement with cattle.

I'm not intimidated by not knowing it. People are willing to tell you, and very helpful. I don't always share a lot of their views. The Department of Agriculture is doing a great disservice promoting chemicals and superphosphate. It's just insanity under the circumstances. So I criticise the Department of Agriculture for that, but on the other hand they do provide a lot of very basic information that people like me find incredibly useful. I did a farm management course through TAFE correspondence school.

I get on really well with Phillip's parents and his other children. I haven't seen a huge amount of them because the eldest one, Rebecca, has been studying at university and now she lives in California, so we correspond. She has visited a few times and we get on very well. Megan, who is twenty-four, I have only gotten to know in the last couple of years and the third one, Saskia, I know less as she lives in Melbourne. Divorce, no matter how much you want to make it a reasonable, rational experience, is never easy. It is always a very hurtful, sad ending. Marriages always start off with such high hopes.

Cameron has continued his career as a film and television composer in the US. I think he has remarried. We kept in touch for a while. Women always want to have friendship after divorce; men never want to have friendship. When I was a teenager and in my early twenties when feminism was the big F-word, I was much more uncompromising. I always wanted to push the idea of getting men to talk about things. I wanted to bring out the female side in men, getting them to communicate more, to talk about the emotional side. Now it's not such a big thing with me. Now I live with someone who communicates easily, although I do think his emotional side is different from mine. I just think it's a different way of looking at the world and I am not trying to bend him and change him all the time. I did a lot of that with Cameron, and I wanted him to be reasonable and rational when I left. Obviously it hurt him a lot. It was not a good time for us, and it was awfully sad. I just wish the best for him. Phillip and I don't intend to marry.

He loves sharing in the experience of the farm but he is not really interested in the daily running. I don't look at it as my thing; I look at it as our thing. I try to get all the grimy stuff done during the week and then on the weekends we can enjoy it. Sometimes I think he's got the best of both worlds. But I don't think I'd swap his life for mine. I'd have to change my personality to swap, because some people can hand everything over to the accountant, but there are other people who have to know that the bank has been reconciled that month—well, I am one of those. I have to know and control all the details. I know where every dollar goes.

Penny-pinching is a good thing on the farm. It's so easy for it to blow out and be endlessly expensive. I like having my finger on the pulse. It's true that Phillip's a lot wealthier than me, but I would have been one of the highest paid women in the country when I was on TV. The amount of money I was able to take away from that, having managed it properly, now makes me a wealthy women in my own right. It's not millions, but it's enough to make me feel very secure. If Phillip died or I met someone else or he said 'I've changed my mind'—heaven help me if that happens, but financially I'd be all right. It's not a worry. I know I'd always survive; that belief in myself will never be destroyed.

Just as I was about to leave, Phillip Adams came bursting through the door carrying their daughter, Rory, at arm's length. He raced past us, shouting, 'She has just done the most enormous poo! How can so much come out of such a little body? I'll deal with it, but you owe me two after this!'

Patrice just looked at me and laughed. It was that Macleans smile.

Driving to the airport in the taxi, I thought of all the money that I and millions of other women have spent and continue to spend on clothes. How wonderful just to choose to wear a clean shirt and a pair of jeans and put that money into securing economic independence for yourself. No wonder she exudes confidence and a strong sense of control. I made a vow to buy fewer clothes and be a lot tighter with my money. Somehow the thought was very liberating.

Rosemary Tipiloura

I attempted to contact Rosemary through her husband Senator Bob Collins's office. Senator Collins's staff told me that she usually declined interviews. I asked if she could ring me so that I could explain the purpose of the book. Time and again I had confronted this difficulty in just getting to talk to the person I wanted to interview.

One night at about ten o'clock the phone rang. 'I'm Rosie Tipiloura—they tell me you want to put me in a book.'

After I had chatted to her for about ten minutes, she said, 'I'll think about it and let you know.' When she agreed about a week later, I caught a plane to Darwin as soon as I could.

The arrangement was that Rosemary would pick me up at my hotel and that we'd go somewhere to do the interview. I waited in the foyer and when Rosemary arrived she said, 'I thought we'd go to the Botanic Gardens; it's cool there and the kids can play where I can keep an eye on them.' It was an inspired choice. Unused to the Darwin heat, I loved the lush coolness of the gardens and in between Robbie going off to play tennis and Libby and Daniel running around, Rosemary told me how she came to be sitting there with me and the children at this point in her life.

MY name is Rosemary Tipiloura-Collins. It was Bob's idea when we got married. He said, 'Stick to your own name. That's how people know you.' I was born on Bathurst Island on 10 November 1954 and lived there until I was fourteen, when I went to Sacred Heart College in Adelaide.

We led a very traditional Aboriginal life. It was a large family and we did a lot of things together, like hunting. It was a Catholic mission, so they separated the men from the young women. At that time they had some problems with some of the older men having three or four wives. We lived in a dormitory situation; my mother was with us. I had two sisters and five brothers, but as I was the oldest I was always expected to be the responsible one, the one they all relied on. By the time I went to Adelaide they had started to phase out the separation of the men from the women. There was still a notion of arranged marriages. I once asked Mum about me and she reckoned I wasn't promised to anybody. Her brothers, as she calls them in the Aboriginal sense, asked her if one of their sons could marry me and she used to have the biggest arguments about it. Once I went down south to Adelaide I was free from all that.

As the eldest I spent a lot of time looking after the other kids. Mum was busy having children and Dad was a sort of gardener-handyman around the shop on Bathurst Island. Mum would be about fifty-eight now. She has had a tough life. She misses Dad a lot. He was drowned in 1990 in a boating accident in the Apsley Strait, which is between Bathurst and

Melville Islands about a hundred kilometres north of Darwin. There were too many people in the boat and it capsized. Five people drowned, including my dad, and one was a baby. The mother saved herself, but was too drunk and hopeless to save the baby. It was very tragic.

That's why I hate drinking. There's too much of it. They get over the limit and don't know when to stop. I can't stand even the smell of beer. A lot of Aboriginal women have encouraged the men to go to AA.

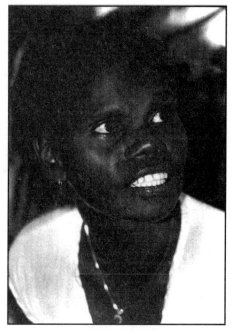

I'm very grateful to the nuns who encouraged me to go to Adelaide to further my education. It was like a scholarship. Five were selected but only two went. Sister Theresa Marie asked me if I would like to go down, and I was billeted with people who used to work at Bathurst. I had no problem with Mum and Dad; even though they didn't understand white culture, they're sensible. Once you explain things to them in simple English, they're fine. I thought I would like to see the big city and what it was like, all those bright lights and noises, TV and radio. If I was scared of going I wouldn't have gone. It was like a sense of adventure, going to another place—another planet almost.

Five of us thought we were smart as we would finish our work first, and the older kids who didn't finish theirs used to punch us up if they wanted answers. I pushed myself into it. I just wanted to learn. I didn't know that I wouldn't have been here and been where I am without it.

When I arrived in Adelaide, I promised myself that if ever I had a family I would never send them away. It took me about two, three months to really get over the loneliness. It wasn't so much loneliness as homesickness. I cried every night. The lady that looked after me was lovely. She still is; I try and keep in touch with her.

The other girl, Cabrini, who was selected, went to Mercedes. Unfortunately, she had cervical cancer and died about two to three years ago. We kept in touch; I would ring her up. But the first whole year in Adelaide we didn't get to see each other. Nowadays children who are boarding are allowed to go home for holidays every so often. But for the whole three years I didn't go anywhere, not even home.

I forgot how to speak in Tiwi. The lady and her husband that I was staying with found out that another girl from Bathurst was going to school in South Australia She managed to get Cabrini to come over for the weekend to my place and vice versa. We would laugh when we used to try to talk in Tiwi and made mistakes. We said, 'It's going to be terrible when we get back home—so embarrassing that we didn't know how to speak our own language.' When I first went back, Mum and Dad and the kids used to talk to me in Tiwi and I didn't have a clue what they were saying. After a while it came back to me—but I was talking back in English to them. That only lasted a couple of months.

When I returned home it was like going from here to Pakistan and not knowing anybody there. I knew all my family, but they looked at me differently. They envied me for being down there but they didn't like it, because I'd changed and they didn't like the change. Cabrini and I were the first to make the breakthrough. We didn't last long on the island because the nuns wanted us to be teachers or health workers. We were qualified to study so they sent us to Kormilba College for community students. It was like TAFE. Both of us found it really easy and not challenging. We knew we were going backwards instead of forwards. We went back to Bathurst to teach for a little while, but that didn't last long. It was so boring. I said to Cabrini, 'I think we should go to Darwin and look for a job.' I was more or less tempting her to come with me, as I didn't want to go to Darwin on my own, and Darwin was closer than Adelaide.

We landed in the right place at the right time, because when we got there this bloke approached us and asked if we were looking for a job. We were staying at the YMCA at that time and they said, 'Come for an interview.' The following day we started working.

The CES had opened a branch called the Aboriginal Employment Service; there were only about three or four people. They said, 'Are you interested?' and we said, 'Yes, no worries.' I worked there for about ten years until I got sick of it. I had to go to outstations and fringe camps around Darwin like Manton Downs and Knuckey's Lagoon. I just helped them fill in unemployment benefits forms. In those days all they did was put a cross, and you did the rest and witnessed the signature. I put young people on training here in Darwin, and then followed it up, and that was how I met Bob. He was supervising their training, and I had to liaise with him about how they were going if they had any problems and so on. We would go to the employer to ask how they were going, and if there was a problem we had to chase the people and bring them back. I got sick of that.

When I met Bob I was in my early twenties. Once we got ourselves established we stayed at the Baptist Hostel. It was all right. After a while we moved to rented flats. I was still with the same girl, Cabrini Pilaku, and a couple of other Aboriginal kids. We all worked together. I was just going on from day to day, intent on having a good time. I looked forward to Fridays, which was payday, when we would go out and have a rage. We would go to dancing, to disco clubs, have a wild time, get drunk, spend the next day with a hangover and wonder if it was worth it.

In 1977 while I was working with the CES, I went to the task force at the SAIT campus in Adelaide. I went down there for a year, but I was stupid—I didn't finish it. I could have if I'd wanted to but I was having too good a time. It brought all the old memories back; I felt Adelaide was my second home. It was my best time. I experienced a lot of things like drugs. I tried them out of curiosity. I wondered why people got a kick out of them. I tried everything. By that time Bob said he had given up on me because he thought I was going to be a drug addict. He wasn't really in the picture for me at that stage.

I had other boyfriends, just casuals, no-one serious at that time. I always thought that if I was going to seriously go with someone I would go a little longer, like two or three months, to get to know the person. That was probably because of my Catholic upbringing. My parents were always very supportive of me.

I have always supported my family in every way I can and still do. They have been really great. They take it in turns to come and see me; if they have a feeling or premonition that something is wrong they would come over. They are all still over at Bathurst. One of my sisters is living in Darwin; she's married to a white man—they've got five children.

I experienced a lot of racism growing up. I still experience racism, but I'm stronger now. When I first came to Darwin I used to be in tears when it happened. I couldn't handle it. I won't take any nonsense now. For example at a shop if we don't get service I say to my kids, 'We'll go to another shop and get better service—my money's clearly not good enough.' And then I say loudly, 'Remind me not to come to this shop ever again.'

I'm not scared to make a scene. I won't take nonsense from anyone. I had a bad experience once down in Adelaide. We went to a disco and they wouldn't let us go in there and I said to them, 'Isn't our money good enough to go in there?' As it was they were charging us $15 extra than the normal rate and I said, 'I'm not going to waste my money on you, I'm going to go somewhere else where I can have a good time.' I felt I had to make a scene before I left. After that the manager said, 'Come in' and apologised for the rudeness and I said, 'No, I'm not going to waste our money.'

Sometimes I ignore it, but if I'm in a bad mood I let them have it. My kids experience it. One time Robbie came home and said, 'One of the kids said I've got a black mum,' and I said,' You go back to school and tell them you've got a black mum that loves you so much. Ask him does his mother love him as much as I love you.' So he told them and he came home and said, 'I told that boy and he didn't answer, so maybe his mother doesn't love him.'

I'm close to my kids. They show a lot of love and affection to me and I do the same to them. We can be in the middle of a crowd of people and they come up and cuddle me and kiss me and say 'I love you' and I always respond in the same way. They are close to their father, too, but he is away all the time with his job.

Anyhow, I decided that trying drugs was ridiculous. I didn't get anything out of it and was appalled at some of the things people did under its influence. So I left Adelaide and came back to Darwin. I was mixing mostly with whites and eating vegetarian meals. I had joined a cult when I was in the task force. I liked it, but didn't see any future in becoming a cult member. It was some sort of religious cult that practised transcendental meditation. It was basically being a hippy. That phase passed and I thought, 'I'm not getting anywhere. I have to find some way of settling down.'

I was looking for security more than anything. I knew that I wanted a secure future, and I wanted to get married, but not to a no-hoper. Every day when I was working I would see young girls my age, drinking and selling themselves for money at pubs. I only went to pubs on Fridays and looked forward to discos, but I couldn't see myself in their shoes. I said to myself, 'I'm never going to be like them. No way.' I decided not to drink. Cabrini went back home; she had a drinking problem. We went through a lot of hard times and sad times together, but there's a lot of happy memories, too. I think about her every now and then. Sometimes when I'm out on my own I think about her. Three other friends have died throughout the year, and every now and then my mind flashes back to them.

I say to my kids, 'You're lucky you don't have a drunken mum.' We've got a strict rule in our house—no drinking. Bob doesn't drink. I smoke and he doesn't. I gamble and he doesn't. I don't know how we are compatible. He has more patience with me than I have with him; I think I'm a typical Scorpio.

So when I came back from Adelaide, I was looking for another job. I was still a sort of hippy. I wanted to travel to Malaysia and Indonesia and had to save some money. I thought I would get two jobs at the same time, save money and plan this trip. For some reason Bob heard from another friend of ours that I was looking for a job. He was the member for Arnhem then. He said, 'I've got a job if you're interested.' At first I was nervous being in the office, him being a Member of the Legislative Assembly, but that didn't last long.

I was grateful, I wanted a job so badly. After about a week I was still working one night and he said he was going out to get a Chinese meal. He said, 'Do you like Chinese?' I was still trying to get my typing right.

There was a large table, him one side and me the other, and he had set out this Chinese meal with a candle and I thought, 'This looks a bit suss.' At that time I wasn't serious about a relationship with anybody. So we were sitting there eating and he suddenly says to me, 'Rosie Tipiloura, I have been in love with you for five years.' I laughed. Poor thing. He didn't know how to react. I said, 'Are you serious?' and he said, 'Yes.' He said, 'I was about to give up.' He had never even asked me out. He had sort of followed my moves and knew I was into drugs and things like that. So we had a feed; then he took me home, and nothing was said. I thought to myself, 'Now, there's a sensible man; I could have a future with him. He doesn't drink or smoke.' And that was when we started our relationship. I was renting a flat with a friend he knew. Then he proposed. I'd had trouble with girls who were flatting with me. I'd had enough of this when I was with my family. I always had to pay extra board and extra money for food. I'd had a lot of boyfriends but none I considered I would be stable with. I couldn't see a future life with any of them.

At first I wasn't in love with him, but it grew. The first year we were together—living in sin, in Catholic terms—I was going to work. For that year I was sort of like a rebel, a bit restless. He was more mature than I was. He's always more serious than me; he still is. I'm more happy-go-lucky.

I was working, but socially I wanted to go out with my friends and have a good time. I loved dancing and he was the opposite; he was a homebody. He left home when he was fourteen; we're his life. He was really close to his grandmother, but she passed away. He has two sisters and two brothers and he's not really close to them. My family loves him—they adore him. They give him a hard time now and then, but he likes that kind of relationship.

My private life was totally different to his, but the racial difference didn't worry me. My parents knew that I was going to marry a white bloke, anyway. They would have been more surprised if I'd married a black man. There was no-one at Bathurst I wanted to marry; it wouldn't have worked. I couldn't see myself living at Bathurst, but I still didn't really know whether I was coming or going.

I loved home and my family but if I didn't have that attachment with my family I wouldn't have lived nearby. If I moved to Canberra I would be worried sick about Mum and my brothers and sisters. If there was an argument, Mum or Dad would ring me up. I would have to go and sort them out. At one stage four of my brothers were involved in a fight and I went over and sorted them and the other people out. It took me a while to learn how to balance the two worlds. I was regarded as too classy. People used to think, 'She thinks she's too good.' And then they would want my help and would come and talk to me. I think I was a bit of a rebel over at Bathurst, too. I couldn't ever settle down there. I gave some of the nuns and the staff a headache.

If it wasn't for Mum or Dad I wouldn't have had the kind of values about bringing up my kids, or being the way I am. I don't want to take advantage of people—I never have and never will. People take advantage of me sometimes, sometimes even my own people if they're in trouble. It has advantages and disadvantages. It now seems to have balanced out. They have accepted me as I am. It took us all a while.

When I told my parents I was getting married, they were good. I thought my father would get really violent. Once when I had a boyfriend and the other men were teasing him, he went and had a go at him. The bloke said, 'Your father said he was going to get a gun and blow my head off.' I have never forgotten that. Being the eldest, he has always relied on me; he doesn't like people saying things about me. He was really receptive with Bob. He came up and shook his hand—they sat together and talked. That was the first time they had met. All my brothers were sitting around watching and when they saw Dad relax they all gave a sigh of relief. Mum loved him. He talked to her and told her he was a converted Catholic.

Bob was away about a month at a time when we were first married. Even when he's home he's got all these meetings and comes home late. I was still working when I had Robbie and Libby, right up to when I had Daniel. I was working for the Land Council and I worked because I liked it. It kept me occupied and there was a child-minding centre there.

Sometimes now I think there must be something I can do instead of sitting at home doing the same old thing over and over again. But I'm not in a great hurry to go back to full-time work. I would rather do some voluntary work. I don't need the money, but I need to do something different. I have just started with the AIDS Council. They need people badly.

Like Bob, I'm a bit of a loner. I like being on my own reading, doing crosswords and watching TV. I like watching good films, legal ones or thrillers. I can't wait for the day I'll be on my own without the kids, even though they are very special. I have always had a good relationship with Bob. We understand each other.

We don't talk about politics. Very rarely. Only at election times. He asks my advice about who is the best person to be preselected. I take it as it comes. Every election I say, 'I have every confidence that you're going to win.' Sometimes he asks my comments on the overall picture. This year I gave up scrutinising. Not that they need my help, anyway.

Bob goes on his own to cabarets and fund-raisers. Just because I'm married to a politician doesn't mean I have to go to all these parties and functions.

It's not me to go to fundraising. Bob has never, ever put pressure on me to do anything for him. Sometimes I feel guilty. I don't mind at election time. I used to go out to communities to help hand out how-to-vote cards. Bob is always worried; he's pessimistic. Whatever he thinks is always opposite to me. I'm always saying I've got confidence. At other times if I'm a bit worried I tell him what I think, like, 'It's going to be a close one.' He always listens to what I say. If he doesn't agree we have a ding-dong battle but I'm always the last one to have a say.

Bob is more patient with me than I am with him. Sometimes I say, 'I could walk away from this house and pack up and go back home.' He just walks away and when he comes back I've settled down.

I tell him that everything goes wrong when he's away and I'm always the one who takes them out to have good or bad times. When Libby had asthma all night, I used to think, 'I'm going to ring Bob up and annoy him as well.' And I'd do it. Why should I be the only one not to sleep?

I have never gone to the opening of Parliament but I don't worry about him being in Canberra on his own. He's very old-fashioned. I can't picture him being unfaithful. If I was worried about that I would be going to all the functions he goes to. I have a tease every now and then, but only because I like teasing. Robbie was only eight months old when Bob went to Zambia and then the United States for two months. If it was another bloke, he would probably be having a good time. But he's not that type, at least I hope he's not that type. We've been married for fourteen or fifteen years.

I don't know how he feels about me, whether he trusts me.

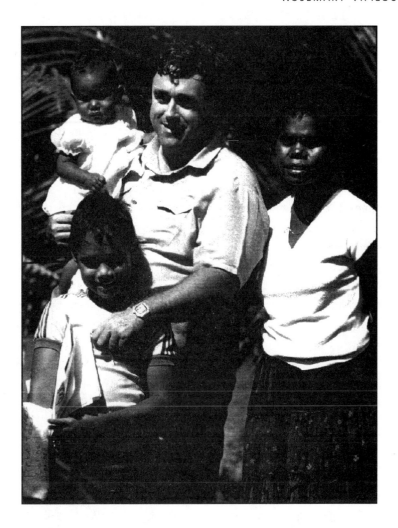

It never occurred to me to play up behind his back, and I can't picture myself playing up, with the kids holding onto my skirts. It's just not my way. But there's been plenty of opportunities.

We are very close with the kids. He very rarely shows love and affection—that's his upbringing. I accept that, just as he accepts my upbringing and the way I treat the kids. He sees them coming up to me more than to him. If he's a bit jealous, he doesn't show it. I was brought up to kiss and cuddle.

He doesn't talk so much about our culture to me, but I hear him telling other people, about how he admires our culture. He knows all the advantages and disadvantages. And he accepts my way. If I'm obligated to go to Bathurst for a funeral or to see someone, he'll send me by plane. My relatives go up to him and cuddle and kiss him. We have a habit of holding people. That's the way we are. For me it's automatic too—sometimes I have to watch myself, especially if I'm talking to a man and hanging onto him. Even though Bob can't show his emotions, he likes the way our culture expresses them.

He often talks to me about having a hard time at work and asks my opinions of people. He's never failed to invite me to any function and even the office rings me up and lets me know about anything. The media is always the worst one, I always say no. I'm sick of people saying they want to interview me because I'm Bob Collins' wife. Why don't they see me for who I am, ask what I have achieved? It might not be much, but at least I've lived my life. They always see me as the minister's wife.

I have never seen myself like that, even when he was Leader of the Opposition in Darwin. People would introduce me as 'the senator's wife'. Sometimes if I got annoyed I'd correct them. I'd say, 'I'm Rosie. I've got a name, I'm a person.' Bob knows that, too. When I get very angry, he says, 'Well, you tell them.'

One time he had a call from a priest who said, 'I got a call from your wife and I'm having a meeting with her. Do you know what it's about? I think I've got a brief idea of what it's about but I want your opinion.' Bob said, 'My wife's opinions are hers—if she makes an arrangement with you it's fine by me; that's her arrangement. It's nothing to do with me.' He treats me as a total equal. He's never put me down. Sometimes I know I act like a five-year-old and am very sarcastic to him when I'm annoyed. Sometimes he drives me mad because he's overprotective. Simple things like, can I catch a plane to Sydney from Darwin and then catch a train from there to his family? I've done that the whole year round and I say to him, 'You think I'm not capable of getting off a train or getting off a plane, organising transport to the railway station and then buying a ticket to take the train to your sister's place?' He likes to organise things, to make sure I'm not hassled. I like being hassled. His staff say, 'He's trying to do you a favour. He loves you.' All that white-car stuff doesn't impress me. I've been there and done that. It's not as if I'm coming from the jungle into a civilised place.

Sometimes I have a go at him about politics. He'll say, 'Right, we'll swap—you take my job and I'll do yours, looking after the kids.' And I say, 'After one day, you couldn't handle them.' I believe that.

After I thought about his first declaration of love I felt guilty. I didn't expect it, especially when I saw all these candles—I'm not the romantic type. Now that he's got me he's not so romantic any more. Sometimes I say to Libby or Robbie, 'Daddy used to open the door for me like the real gentleman he was at one stage. He'd send me flowers on my birthday if he was in Canberra.' He doesn't remember our wedding anniversary; neither of us do. My mother rings to say 'Happy Anniversary' and I think, 'God, it's that time of the year again!'

Bob rings me up every day—never fails. Sometimes two or three times a day. Libby rings him up all the time. She says, 'Can I speak to Senator Bob Collins?' Daniel won't say 'Senator'; he says, 'Is my dad there?' They're good kids on the whole.

I would carry on if Bob died. I can get a job any time if I

want to. Although Bob says there's no need for me to worry about jobs, that we would be financially secure now. But for my own sake I would get a job or study.

I've thought about computers and study even now. I always have Bob's support. He says, 'Whatever you do is fine by me.' If he doesn't agree with what I do he would tell me and I would respect his opinion. But if I really wanted to do something, if I really believed in it, I'd do it.

Whatever happened, I don't think I would ever resort to drinking. It's not me. I hope not, anyway. I see myself as a survivor. If I saw myself as a loser or a no-hoper I wouldn't have ended up where I am now—I would be at the pub drinking every day. It depresses me to see my people living like that. What annoys me most is, if I can do it, so can they. I hate it when people, white people, say to me, 'You blackfellas, you're all the same.' Well, we're not. We're all different individuals. Just because we have black skin we are not all no-hopers. I've never accepted grants or support from anybody. I've always been independent. They've got tertiary schemes for Aboriginal people, housing schemes, education schemes, throwing money at them, and there are all these part-Aboriginal fellows grabbing it. I would rather do it the hard way. I did it on my own without any help.

I give one or two talks a year, perhaps open an art exhibition. I say to them, 'Is it because I'm Bob Collins' wife or do you want me?' I don't have any pressures from Bob or from anybody. If they put pressure on me I tell them to get lost, blacks or whites.

I've always had good responses from people. I sometimes have bad vibes and think I shouldn't have said this or done that. I've now got to be a bit careful of what I say because of Bob. When I was working at the Land Council sometimes people would say, 'Your bloody husband!' or 'I don't like your bloody husband,' and I'd say, 'Well, that's your opinion. You're entitled to your opinion. If you have something to say to him, go and tell him, not me.' I don't see myself as very political but I know enough. I would vote for Bob, even though he's my husband. If I didn't like his ways or values I'd tell him.

Bob was so pessimistic about the last election but I knew Labor would win. I just knew. Sometimes I get premonitions, like if my mum is ill. That's what happened when my uncle Stanley Tipiloura died. The day before we got the news that he'd died I said to Bob, 'I smell death.' I don't like using my intuition much, because it can sometimes be a disadvantage; it can be dangerous. But I said to him, 'I feel no good; I feel like I'm dying.' Bob said, 'What do you mean?' He gets very frustrated with me when I get like that. I told Robbie that the feeling I had was scary; he said it scared hell out of him. I said, 'I don't think it's me, but someone close to me like my nephew or niece, my aunty or uncle.' Other times I would say, 'It will be my sister's kids'—one died of meningitis and I had that sense. We were very close to that little one, too. She was very premature and we would go and see her every night. We got very excited when she got rid of the tube and had a bottle. When she died that really cut me up, even Bob. We were going to take her and feed her up and make her strong and then send her back home to Bathurst. She only lived three months, poor little thing.

Black politics is too radical for me. I stay away from them. I like listening to people like Pat O'Shane; I think she is a very classy lady. But apart from that, that's it. Politics is not me; I can't see myself being like Pat Dobson, Pat Turner or Marsha Langdon. It's them, not me. Sometimes I think, 'What are they trying to prove?' Sometimes I say to myself, 'I don't have to be out in the open saying "I'm Bob Collins' wife" or "I'm

Rosemary Tipiloura." I don't feel the need to tell the world who I am.' I don't like marching, or protesting. It's not me. Why do we have to prove ourselves? My first experience with so-called radical blacks was at Monash University. My girl-friends and I had ordered coffee and were sitting down when these so-called blackfellows came and said, 'Pleased to meet you, sister—brother so-and-so.' I looked at them and thought, 'What the hell is going on?' And my friends were laughing because they know me too well. These people said, 'Would you like to come up to the Aboriginal Resource Centre?' I said to my friends, 'Are they nungas? You could have fooled me.' When I went up there, I couldn't even see anyone the same colour as my children. I felt out of place even though they were trying to make me welcome. I thought they were pho-nies, a mob of fakes. I still think some of them are jumping on the bandwagon. I've always been a loner and done it on my own—never needed my father and mother to give me money. I've supported them.

Sometimes when I hear about people who have rallies down south, or I read it in the newspaper, I think, 'What the hell do they know about living in communities?' Get them to live at Bathurst or Wattie Creek and see what they think of living in a humpy. I'd like people like that to come up and have real ex-perience in the bush. Pat Dodson has been there and done it. But all those radical people go ahead and say things without realising what consequences they have. Simple people in com-munities don't want to be hassled by whites or blacks. They just want to be left alone. I know some of the radicals mean well, but they are not always right.

My kids love going back to see my family. They look for-ward to it. They feel comfortable there. The only thing I don't like is the drinking.

I tell my brothers to go if they arrive at the door very drunk.

I never used to do it. In the last couple of years I've started to be strong. They will probably hate me for it.

I have my own life to lead. My life revolves around the children—we laugh and fight and cry together. We have more fun things together than unhappy things. When Dad died they were really upset. I have a lot of admiration for my children in accepting two cultures.

At home when there are deaths they don't like going to funerals. It's very depressing. They handle it, though. It's taboo to talk about deaths like in my father's case, but I make sure my children don't forget him. Sometimes they forget where they are and which culture they are in. My aunties don't like my children talking about dying with them. I say to them, 'It's okay just in our house, but not in front of Mum.'

I respect my own culture. I feel I'm obligated. I don't know how you determine what's right and wrong in the Aboriginal culture—suss it out, I suppose. Everyone's always happy to see me. We never have arguments and fights with my own people. They talk to me about things that concern them and ask for my opinion. They know where they stand with me. So far I have had a good relationship with my family.

I have power in my marriage with Bob, but Bob is harder on the children and won't let them get away with as much as I do.

I love Bob and I have respect for him. Once when we sent the kids away so we could be alone, it was five days of murder. We were so worried about them. Bob always says his life isn't worth living if he didn't have us. I don't know whether he had other girlfriends before me. He's never told me. He hates me teasing him; he's too straight. Never talks about his private life. I get on very well with his family—they're lovely.

He's come a long way and I admire him for that. The first year he did law by correspondence at Queensland University, all his essays were distinctions. He finished one year but has another four years to go. Politics gets in the way of serious study.

I think Bob would be a gardener if he wasn't a politician. I wasn't looking at him as a politician; I married him because he loved me, but even before that he looked to me like someone who would look after me. It didn't take long to have love for him. Once I had the kids I could see him in them. I have seen a lot of women who have been abused through drinking and I thought, 'No way would that happen to me.' I had a boyfriend earlier who used to play up behind my back and drink. I just dumped him. No way was anyone going to bash me up. I'm a survivor.

The schooling in Adelaide really gave me a lot of confidence. I've got other values, which I get from my family and the nuns. They played a big part in my life also, for which I am grateful.

I believe in God. Hypocrites are the ones who have to go to church on Sundays. Being a practising Catholic you shouldn't have to go to church on Sundays and say rosaries. I go when it suits me. I feel Christmas is a special time, I go to midnight mass, and I go to church on Sunday at Easter. My belief gives me a sense of belonging.

We have Christian friends, Jesuit friends who are very close to us. Bob has three girlfriends who are nuns. They absolutely adore him and he has a lot of admiration and respect for them. They have had a hard life in Bathurst. Sister Ann Gardiner used to teach me when I was little. She knows I don't go to church every Sunday. She's like my second family. I have a lot of respect for them. And so does Bob. When my father died, they held a special mass for him.

Since my dad died I take my kids down to the beach and we talk about it. It's very hard to explain to them about life, especially two lives, white and black, but they learn to balance it.

They say to me, 'How come he drowned when he knew the sea? He was a good sailor.' I never accepted it until later on when I realised he belonged to the sea, it was his way. I wouldn't say that in front of my family; it was a tragic death to them. Aboriginals have a spiritual understanding of such things, but some things must never be spoken. In Tiwi culture you are not allowed to use that person's name for a long time.

In our culture pointing the bone and even promised marriages seem to have faded out. I know initiations are still very strong in Arnhem Land, but I don't know whether they practise it at Bathurst. Women aren't supposed to know, anyway.

I'm frightened of snakes and I'm frightened of dying. But then there's another side to it—curiosity? What's it like to die? My people believe in life after death, and talk about spirits. We still carry on our traditions. When my father died, I felt his presence. It was real.

It's easy for my children to distinguish between the two cultures. If they make a mistake, the older people help them. They don't get cross. My children speak Tiwi and can understand it. They love hunting and crabbing with Mum. The Bathurst boys like showing Robbie what to do. They come around and pick him up. Bob is inclined to be overprotective.

What I'm really looking forward to is eventually studying for a BA. I want to do something very difficult and know that I'll succeed. If I fail I'll keep doing it. I don't care however long it takes, I'll get there. I don't want my people to think I'm a do-gooder, and I think so far I have managed that. I choose to dress normally and not be Lady Muck. That's not me, my personality. I like them to see me as the same old Rosie. It has worked so far. I'll have a racing car or dyed red hair in my old age.

Bob and I don't sit together at football because I scream and make an idiot of myself. It doesn't stop me. Even my sisters get embarrassed. They tell me not to carry on like a mad-woman or an idiot. You can't just sit there and watch the game and not get excited. Bob says I'm deafening and embarrassing. When I say I have a sore neck or a headache afterwards Bob says it serves me right. But if I go to have a good time, I have a good time.

I think Bob and I will stay together. I can picture us in our old age at Wimbledon watching Robbie playing tennis. I often say to Bob after an argument that I can leave any time I want to, but my love is too strong for both my husband and children. I'll begin my adventures when I'm fifty or eighty.

Rosie and I could have gone on talking into the darkness. The kids had been very well behaved but were dying for a drink. We all piled into the car and took off. The two youngest were bright, confident, open and treated their mother with a mixture of respect and friendship.

Rosie told me that she had been invited by Annita Keating to lunch in Canberra at the Lodge.

'Will you go?' I asked her.

'No way.'

'Why not?'

'It's not me.'

'Will you ever go?'

'Maybe once—just out of curiosity,' she laughed. 'I'll choose my time, when I'm ready.'

'But what if by some twist of fate or politics your husband becomes the prime minister?'

'I've told him: he'd be living in the Lodge on his own. I like it here, close to my family.'

I knew she meant it. If she didn't want to go, no amount of persuasion would move her from Darwin to the Lodge. She is first and foremost her own person. She told me quietly that when she gets a chance she loves to go, either with a friend or by herself, to bingo and smoke.

'She loves bingo, but she shouldn't smoke,' chirped Libby.

Rosemary laughed. 'They don't let me get away with anything, this lot.'

When they dropped me off at my motel, Rosie beeped the horn and the kids hung out the window waving goodbye.

In a world where a politician's wife has become almost as trapped in the public spotlight as the politician himself, there is a great deal of pressure to conform to an image of what is expected. It is assumed that such a wife will shape and manoeuvre her life around her partner's political career. So often I have found such women afraid to say what they mean in case the media use it against their partners. So often these women are treated as adjuncts or appendages to their partners and their partners' careers.

In such a world, Rosemary Tipiloura is a refreshing antithesis. Her honesty is her greatest source of strength.

Cherryl Barassi

I'd heard that the wife of Ron Barassi was the total opposite of the so-called 'footie wife'. I rang her up out of the blue, told her about the book and we arranged to meet.

The front bar of the Mountain View Hotel in the Melbourne suburb of Richmond looked at first glance like the front bar of any average Australian suburban pub. I stood there for a moment and looked around.

The woman behind the bar said, 'You're not selling red noses, are you?'

'No. I'm here to do an interview.'

Cherryl Barassi introduced herself and held out her hand. Her grip was firm and forthright. She smiled and said, 'I've got nothing against SIDS or people wearing red noses, but the only cause I really care about, the only cause that really counts in the end, is population control.'

She went on immediately to introduce the bloke behind the bar as her 'non-biological son', and asked me what I'd like to drink. We settled on a bottle of Killawarra champagne and I followed her downstairs to the basement area, usually reserved for dining. We sat at a table, poured the champagne and let it rip. She told me she had agreed to do the interview, not only because she liked the sound of me over the phone, but because she had also checked me out with some of her media mates. The only time we were interrupted in the ensuing hours was by her non-biological son's offer of coffee.

IN retrospect I think I was the luckiest child I've ever met. My sister and I had parents who were civilised, we had good books in the house, which I think should be essential for everybody, and they did not tell us any misinformation. We weren't indoctrinated, we weren't forced to have dolls or grow up on the *Women's Weekly* plan. Such an upbringing was very rare. I think they were too busy really to be too heavy with us.

I went to fourteen schools; my sister may have even gone to more. A couple were in New South Wales just over the border, several out of the city and then mostly coming back to St Kilda in between other jaunts. I was born in St Kilda and they were St Kilda people. My entrepreneurial grandfather, an old Jewish fellow with a nose like a light globe, kept coming up with creative ideas and dragging my father around after him to rescue him. That involved having an orchard, a pub, real estate, a gun shop, a fishing shop and all kinds of things which we lived on the fringe of, and therefore we had a lot of freedom. I asked my mother recently why she had not taught me how to cook the way she does and she said, 'I could never find you.'

We grew up with our own horses and rifles. My father would make sure I had a clean handkerchief, ten bob and a knife, all tied up my sleeve. The money was called panic money and I was not asked what time I would be home. As a result we were quite responsible, capable young people who really did not get into trouble.

We learned to be self-reliant, but with a marvellous sense of security. I never saw my parents drunk or fighting, or sneering or being unreasonable. It's hard to imagine planning it any better, really.

I always wanted to be an artist. I wanted to make animated cartoons through my childhood and my teenage years, but went straight into the typing pool out of commercial school at the age of sixteen. Although I was offered an art scholarship from secondary

school, my father and I agreed that it would be better to have some sort of diploma of commerce to last me for life, because realistically you can't expect to make a living in art—it's in the luxury area.

After I had worked for a few years part-time, I went to art school. It was a time of hard-edge painting and I didn't relate to it. I really wanted to learn the skills of the craft because I felt the rest would be up to my imagination. I was very disappointed with the standard of art schools, around 1968. I lasted all of a year there and went back to work, painted for my own pleasure and drew as I always had done and still do.

I have been involved in mixed shows, but I have never had a solo exhibition. The sort of work I like to do is better done on consignment, because my materials are very expensive. I like doing four-panel dressing screens on perspex in brass grains. It is about $500 to put one together, and if you get a Toorak matron saying, 'I love that but I wish it had more blue,' you would be better knowing that in the beginning. I have had commissions of that kind.

I remember my father asking me when I was about twenty if I was a lesbian. It was an amazing question to me, because I wasn't but I didn't want to preclude that. I didn't want children and I didn't expect to get married, so I said, 'I am without prejudice.'

I had not been indoctrinated and therefore I was free to choose. He did say to me once, 'A woman without children is like a tree without blossoms,' and I said, 'Perhaps I'm an oak tree and I am just going to have a few nuts around me through my life.' We were very shy breeders; neither my sister nor I have ever wanted children. I never had a moment's hesitation about it. Although I must admit, I almost lactate around small animals. You can always borrow children; your friends are very happy to lend you some. People try to save their marriages with babies; they think, 'This will complete us' and of course it won't.

Because I was easygoing and a fairly level-tempered person I was quite attractive to men. I had lots of friends and boyfriends and dates. I am in my second marriage now. I was married to a rock-and-roll singer from Adelaide when I was twenty-four. At the time I was managing rock-and-roll groups and singers and doing some stage presentation, but I was never tempted to become a singer myself. They were a bit suburban up close and their egos were out of balance, so I didn't want to be like that at all. He was gorgeous, very attentive and very kind, and at that age you can fall in love quite easily. It was my first really interesting sexual encounter, and so I thought I must be in love. I have seen him recently; he is still a nice man. We are friends, but we have absolutely nothing in common. They are the questions you don't ask when you're that age.

I left him at twenty-seven. He was from Adelaide and I followed him back there and got a job managing the North Adelaide Art Gallery. We lived there for a few years and there was absolutely nothing happening between us. He had a very good band; whenever there was a visiting star performing they would use them as musicians.

Eventually I said to him, 'I am very miserable. If you can do anything about it I will give you six months to see what you can do about it, or I am off.' I left almost six months to the day, on good terms. I even left him a week's worth of ironed shirts. I went back to Melbourne, to my friends and family. I love Melbourne. I didn't think I had failed. I thought he was a failure. I had tried hard, and I think I was a terrific and co-operative person to live with. Once he realised that I was wrong there and with him, the sexual attraction went quite quickly. Men need to feel pretty good and confident and unthreatened to keep being a sex symbol.

I think I threatened him intellectually, but I certainly did not mean to. The qualities I like in people have nothing to do with their socio-economic status, but it does have something to do with spirit and courage and goodwill, and that can come from anywhere.

I have had about thirty-six jobs in my life. I've always had a bit of graphic art work, textile design work, but that's spasmodic so you can't count on it for a living. I am quite proud of the fact that I've only worked part-time for the period after my first marriage until now. It's been enough for me to live on. I'm quite happy to rummage round in op shops for my clothes and worldly belongings; in fact I enjoy it. I could live in one room with good company and a bottle of cooking sherry quite happily—good company being the priority. I don't need a car—I have a bicycle. I don't really need much at all—I am not into jewellery or facials, and I can cut my own hair.

When I returned to Melbourne I worked for an advertising agency; then I worked for Tom Lazar. That was a beaut job and very educational. Tom and I are still friends. I like him; he's a mad Hungarian and a very exciting person. We'd do a bit of aerobatics in his Tiger Moth in the morning, we might prune some vines up at his property, then entertain extraordinary people for lunch and then we would work fairly hard.

My mother's grandmother was an Aborigine and my mother's part-Jewish and my father's side was entirely Jewish with different nationalities. Belle Jervis, my great-grandmother, was locked in a woodshed in Wagga and forced to marry one of the Jervis blokes from one of the very powerful white families from Jervis Bay. She was an extraordinary woman. She left him after having two children, had a herbalist practice in Collins Street, was the first woman in Melbourne to have a car, was a vegetarian, was in gaol twice for being a suffragette and a spiritualist, and only wore silk next to her skin. My mother remembers her. She lived several years in China and brought back herbal remedies. She wore tinted glasses and was an extraordinary woman to be at the top of Collins Street. I can't tell you how amazing it was in those days to think of a woman doing these things.

In the photographs she is clearly black. She didn't live to a ripe old age, but was an opinionated woman, who chained herself to the gates of Parliament House. She had people coming from as far as Japan for her herbal remedies. She was the first person in Melbourne to have a type of radiography machine, that puts an electric current over skin. I don't think she was ever divorced. She lived with a woman who was her amanuensis who would lay her silk underwear out every day and keep her Chinese antiques perfectly dusted and waxed. It sounds like Alice B. Toklas and Gertrude Stein to me, but who can we ask now? I don't value genetics overly, but it is very interesting ancestry to have. My sister Julie Copeland is apparently quite like her as a type, according to my mother and other relatives. I think they view me as a sunny sort of a character to have around, who is always very helpful in a tight spot.

I have never had a credit card or a bill in my life and I don't want to. Never had a debt. I am just trying to stay out of the system. I did apply for a credit card once and I was knocked back because I had never had a bad debt. I do without or I save up. I could be in gaol now, if I had done what the good old boys did in the Eighties. I bought a tiny house on a tiny deposit in Adelaide and sold it at about 300 per cent profit. That money has always kept me going. I have had such a lot of terrific experiences that I haven't really needed a lot of money.

I travel lighter than anyone I have ever met. I've been overseas for ten weeks with one small suitcase. I have some friends who take their foot massager for overnight stays. I would take my satchel overnight. It is probably my Aboriginal heritage.

'Mabo, Schmabo' is a Jewish Aboriginal thing to say, but I would much rather have the Aboriginals looking after the environment than the expatriate Europeans that have stuffed it up over these 200 years. I certainly didn't feel different as a child. We don't look particularly Aboriginal. It was of no consequence.

Lazar's was a hard act to follow. I went to work for an advertising agency in a secretarial role, which was part-time because I always wanted to be free to paint or do the things that I enjoy. Ormsby Wilkins was the talkback king of Melbourne and when I left Lazar he offered me a job working with him, but my sister then took over as his producer. He is probably the best friend I have ever had in my life. We travelled overseas a couple of times and we would always be the last to leave a restaurant, could not stop talking to each other. He introduced me to so many people, overseas and here. It was such a broadening experience and he was always so supportive and appreciative; just the best person for my morale.

It's a magical thing to have a friend who is powerful, can offer you entrée and appreciate you on your own terms. It was a strange relationship, but he talked me into agreeing to get married, although it was a platonic relationship. He said, 'You're never going to want to marry or have children; let's live in the same house and have a life together.' I could see why that might work with him because we never did bore each other. We really were a boon to each other's lives.

My sister came back from Europe because my father started dying of cancer in '73. She had been overseas for fourteen years, so I did not really know her and I was really keen to meet her. Ormsby had an operation on the 11 November 1975, the day the Labor Party was thrown out of office, the day of Ned Kelly's death, lest we forget, plus the day my father died. It was a boomer of a day. Then we had the news that Ormsby's cancer was inoperable and that he would be coming back to our house to die as well.

That Christmas, a month later, Ron Barassi came to visit Ormsby at our house and he had just been thrown out of his first marriage. I didn't know him, but we did have a bit of chemistry when we checked each other out. My sister and mother had said, 'What would you like for Christmas?' and I'd said, 'A new man who knows nothing about this horror stretch we have been through. Just a totally new experience.' So Ron arrived on my doorstep as my Christmas present, I think.

Later on he invited me out to dinner and I went. He was just out of his marriage, I was preparing for Ormsby's death and my father had just died. We did not talk a lot. I thought he would never bother to see me again, but in fact we were good company because we were both grieving for our various reasons. That went on for a couple of months and I did not get my non-biological children until a year later.

Ormsby was on radio with Claudia Wright in that period of wonderful radio for Melbourne. She has Alzheimer's disease now and she doesn't recognise us when we visit; she is in a very bad state. She was a colleague of Ormsby's and I was a fan of hers. I met her several times, but she was a star in those days and pretty impatient with anyone who was not as powerful as she. My sister was producing Ormsby, but when he died she swapped over and produced Claudia and they became the closest of friends.

Someone had tipped Ron off that Ormsby's and my relationship was an odd one, so he felt entitled to ask me out, but he did check first. Ron doesn't spend any time in reflection. He is a true renaissance man. He's zen in the art of everything, which is both frustrating and inspiring.

I thought he was pretty special. He was such a terrifically energetic-looking creature, independent and roguish and above all playful, which is a lovely quality. When we started getting a bit involved and took each other more seriously, he said he wouldn't be interested in getting involved with someone who wanted a family, as he already had one. I said, 'I haven't a family and I don't want a family, so that's not going to be an issue with us.'

Shortly afterwards when we started living together I had his three children land on the doorstep, one after the other, and I rarely saw Ron. He was busy fishing himself out of a bankruptcy problem, and worked like a machine all day and all night for a year or more. He would ring me from places in Western Australia where he was doing talks and say, 'Do you know where such-and-such is?' and I'd say no and he would say, 'Neither do I, but I'm there.'

His children liked me and liked living in the city. They were just at an age where they wanted to have a bit more of a high time and I was probably more like an older sister, not being at all maternal.

Ron is nine years older than me. The children are a credit to their parents—I suspect mostly their mother—because they all wanted to do the right thing, which is a very good place to start with children.

I was working for an advertising agency part-time and doing my own art work. When my father was dying for three years I was the mainstay, being the only driver in the family. That meant two trips a day to Warburton because he would not eat the food and we didn't want him to. That's a very demanding experience—I am sure most people know about it.

My mother coped wonderfully, but we were a small family and, not having kids, we looked like being the end of the branch of the tree. We were very loyal to her and she had gone a bit ratty. She had us constantly repainting her house in a different shades of colours. We would be whispering to each other, 'We have painted this, but it doesn't matter—paint it again.' That's how we survived—we renovated. Women are good at that.

When Ron and I moved in together I found a house I liked in St Kilda and began a huge renovation. It had mushrooms growing out of the wall at head height, but it was a bargain. I don't like getting in debt. I wish Ron felt the same.

Ron was the only man I could have lived with, because he

was rarely home. It was nothing like a normal relationship. I was always pleased when I saw him and we would have news for each other. By being playful and positive and courageous we skimmed through the early stages of a relationship. I was unencumbered in every way, so I didn't bring any problems to him. He was the encumbered one and I helped more with solving his problems.

As a Konrad Lorenz fan I am interested in animal behavioural science and I know nothing about children. So I applied animal behavioural science and it worked like a charm; I would give that advice to anybody. Children like to know their limitations; they feel much more secure when they know exactly what they can and can't do around you and that you have entitlements too. Being a step-parent is different to being a parent because you can say, 'I am not bonded to you, but luckily I do love you and wish you well. I will back you up, but I won't put up with any shit.'

One night Ron came home and I had Richard, the younger child at the age of about fourteen, by the throat in the hall, up against the wall saying, 'I don't want to have to beat the shit out of you, Richard.' I won't tell you what he had been doing. Ron said, 'You can't speak to the children like that,' and I said, 'Of course I can! They are just little animals; they know what I am talking about.' And they did. They like me and trust me and the feeling is mutual.

It was pretty ideal for Ron. He didn't eat a meal out of bed for eleven years if he was home. A tray in bed and being appreciated and spoilt is a pretty good life. It's a pleasure for me to do that for people I care for. Not so much a sultan as a sultana. He is totally undomesticated, and so when he visits or when he is around he gets spoiled.

In the early days I'd see him perhaps three times a week, which seemed pretty perfect to me. He fished himself out of debt, to his credit, just through sheer hard work. He began coaching and continued his life. He is the perfect commander type. He never says thank you or sorry and I think they are leadership prerequisites. It wouldn't suit the average person to live around someone like that. He is unsupportive at a personal level. I don't need it as much as most. I get it from others. I have always valued my friends above my lovers, always.

I have heard that it's possible to get your lover and best friend in one person, but I have never actually seen that happen. We got married after six years. It was very secret and quiet. I have a couple of gay friends up in the hills who are landscape gardeners so their house doesn't have a primary colour and their garden is exquisite. It was a perfectly sunny day, there were a dozen people there—very immediate family—and the prettiest wedding I've ever seen.

The celebrant had a divergent squint, so it was very hard to look her in the eye and that was making Ron and me laugh a lot, so the photographs are really very funny. Just before the ceremony she said, 'I must tell you that Ron singlehandedly put my husband out of office in the local council elections.' How hilarious!—just before she was to marry us she tells me that Ron had ruined her life.

Getting married had a lot to do with renovations and paying bills. Having separate names kept complicating bookwork. I was attending to so much of Ron's business by this stage that if I was signing cheques in another name they would keep coming back and questioning. It just seemed to be a more practical thing to do at the time. I didn't feel a need to be married; I don't think Ron did, either. We would propose to each other from time to time but he would look at his diary and couldn't on that day or I'd have changed my mind on another day. That went on for a long time.

When I met Ron I asked what team he played for and he

hadn't been playing for years. I knew and I still know nothing about football. I had never heard Ron talk about football socially and still haven't. People talk to him about it, but with a reasonable person he can swerve them away from that.

He reads biographies and autobiographies; he loves current affairs; he loves politics. I think he's a right-wing fascist and he things I'm a Commie poofter and introduces me as such to politicians. He said to Michael Hodgeman, the mouth from in the south, 'This is my wife and Commie poofter.' I held my hand out thinking, 'Thank you, Ron,' and he withdrew his hand—I don't know if he thought he would get AIDS. We're a funny match.

At the bottom line our ethics are the same. It's not morals, because we don't like sentiment. It's a human invention, sentiment; I don't even respect it as an emotion. It's a word that people use when they can't feel love. Most men are sentimental because they haven't accessed their right brain, so sentiment is the best they can do. Ron is capable of love; he is just not too good at expressing it verbally or in his actions. I know it's there because you get an amazing wave of goodwill and acknowledgement if that's what you need to do or want to do. It's like, 'I trust you, I love you and go ahead and do it.' He's never inhibited my freedom and he's tried to let me be myself, which is his best expression of love, I think.

In terms of fidelity, the good news for women involved with top sportsmen is, they don't have as much to prove as the average bloke. There's a flirt at every party, but I wouldn't have been involved with a man who was promiscuous. A bit of 'happenstance' can happen to anyone and it wouldn't ruin my marriage or my life either way, but neither of us seem to have that tendency. We have had talks about it. Life's very short, and if a bit of happenstance comes your way, then I don't want to know the gory details. I wish him to have a full and happy life; if that includes a few adventures, fine, but I would never have him doing it on my time or at my expense. We do agree that if we are out socially together we find flirts pretty pathetic because they're looking for victims and it's so unscrupulous. We don't victimise each other at all. He is like old hessian underpants. He is as butch as the iron jock strap; it's amazing. He's so completely undomesticated—had to ask me after eleven years where the fuse box was, darling.

It is a bizarre combination. I have never met anyone easier to live with. He's squeaky clean—had only to have explained once the reasons for putting the toilet seat and lid down and it was down ever after. He's very trainable.

I do the washing and ironing, but actually only dust my stove. I haven't cooked for two years, literally. Our hours and our lifestyle are so odd. I would be very happy to get up out of bed at eleven-thirty at night and cook Ron a meal—and I mean totally happy about that. He would need it and couldn't do it himself and I could. I never thought to teach him to cook; I sensed it was a hopeless cause.

I still like and respect Ron, probably more than I ever did, and I am old enough to value that more highly than almost anything. His courage and his sense of fun are such redeeming qualities that where I may want to kill him at least once a week I am very glad I didn't at least once a week. I suppose that's the balance you end up hoping for.

Because we're independent people our wills clash. We are used to running our own shows. Probably because I'm a woman I'm more co-operative; because he's the man, he's more competitive. I think it's biological. I love that male energy; I just wish they were educated enough to channel it in a constructive way. I haven't met a man who's done that.

It's a passionate relationship, in that we have eyeball-to-eyeball confrontations at the same intensity. It developed into a good sexual thing, but we weren't twenty when we met, we were thirty and thirty-nine. You are not simply being led around by your hormones. He is a very nice, healthy, physical creature. But if you tie his hands down he can't speak—he's still Italian. At our age the hormones have let go of the throat fractionally and the brain has started to engage and you can hold people to account on your own terms. I can't imagine anything that would be a worry because we are both pretty open. I'm involved with Ron's life every waking minute because we are now working together full-time; it's my first full-time job, really.

We still live on the Esplanade in St Kilda in the house I wanted to live in since I was seven. We bought the house on April Fool's Day. Ron was at the football and I took a mate of mine along to do the bidding because they already knew that Ron was interested in it, so they would have upped the price. I put a couple of stooges in the audience and we bought it at a ridiculous price—mind you, it was just a shell. It's a wonderful place to live. Before it was trendy you could park your car and have friends home. Ron would just drop in and out and supervise the renovations and as soon as he would leave the workmen would ask me what I wanted done.

I absolutely believe in the left and right brain activity. Almost as soon as I met him, I knew he had an over-developed saurian cortex. The saurian is the dinosaur quality, the reptilian quality. It's a very active part of the human brain and anyone who reaches the top in any sphere is very likely to have a highly developed saurian cortex; I believe that as a scientific fact. I don't believe in myth and magic. I am a realist first and an idealist second.

I wouldn't have minded if he had never achieved anything, but I think I would need someone around me who had that spirit. Everybody likes power because it is energy, but I couldn't support anyone who was directing that energy into something I didn't approve of.

Thank Christ for football, because what would Ron have been without football? He would be a General Patten. There would have to have been football or a war for him to find something into which to channel all his energy. He's a born captain.

I am a very good 2IC, by the look of it. I do continue to fall for the nurturing and the supportive calls. I am sure that is biological, because it wouldn't be the way I would plan my life in cold blood, but it's the way my life goes. I couldn't go past someone close to me needing help and not think that was more important than voting, even.

There are a lot of women I don't count as women. I never counted Margaret Thatcher as a woman; she's playing the male game and I'm very disappointed in women like that. I'm firmly committed to equal rights. If men and women had a left–right brain balance they would come into much more equality. Some days I'm all testosterone, and men are sometimes oestrogen-predominant, but there is a 20 per cent hormone difference and it seems to make an enormous difference in our culture. I know I am generalising, but I think it's a fair generalisation. I do wish for a world where men, because of our culture, would come into some sort of parity with women.

Women seem to be trying for change—men don't.

My main desire is a good result for the planet. I support few causes. I spent a lot of time in the country as a kid, and so I did see the seasons change and I've always had animals. I think anyone with that experience values it.

I am not a joiner; I find rallies embarrassing. Walking down amongst ninety people at the anti-uranium rally that I was dragged along to by my pubic hair, a friend of mine and I were saying, 'Do you think they would give us a group concession to *Yentl*?' We were both embarrassed; we just wanted to get the hell out of there. I can't dress as a chicken and tie myself to the steps of Parliament House. Animal liberation, I think, is the quickest philosophy to bring everything into sanity. If you are not going to be speciesist, sexist or racist then you've got a fair chance of making a good decision. I glossed over feminism. I have to say that anything that seems to me to be truth never comes like news, it comes like an affirmation to an open mind.

I'm certainly tough but I'm not hard. I do feel so much for young people these days. I'm not maternal but I can't imagine what it's like to live with a holocaust of this magnitude over your head when you're young. It must be so desolate.

If I hear anyone talking about their rights any more I am going to barf. In this country where everybody, roughly speaking, has a roof over their head and enough to eat, or is looked after, that puts us under 5 per cent of the people of the world. If you can also read and write and have the freedom to choose, you get down to 1 per cent of people on the planet. If that reality was brought home more strongly, people would realise that with that comes an enormous responsibility.

I feel it greatly, but I'm not going to the rallies. I am not a joiner. I work in my immediate sphere of life. We have to do something about overpopulation on this planet. This is something I am truly passionate about.

I have always had access to being heard because of the good fortune of my background and my ability to stand alone and articulate. I have always been able to have influence, and I have always had such an interesting and varied lot of friends. It does in effect become a fairly influential group in the community, although it's not a power-crazed group.

I am a political person, but I'm not involved in politics and don't want to be. I do support groups who will change legislation; I support lobby groups that have the ability to go the long hard road to change legislation, and I do barrack for them. I think it would be detrimental to me to put my energy into being there.

I have never won with Ron, never. It won't stop me clashing with him. I'm not aggressive but I'm strong in defence.

It's commitment and energy that binds me to him. When I think I'm not in love with him or I'm about to kill him, I've happened along to one of his talks and thought, 'Can this be this bit of old furniture around the house that I call Ron and here he is inspiring me?' It's that inner self that is very honest, that is very courageous, that emanates. It's inspiring, and that's why I don't kill him or leave him. There is no crime in Ron; if I saw any crime in him I would kill him.

Ron's commitment to the national game is intense and I think as a chess player he's read it right. If they don't hold Sydney as part of this chess game, then you might as well kiss football goodbye. It is the most populated city in Australia and it's a marvellous game for those who like it. I certainly don't.

I've been to the football once with Ron, and I've never been so bored in my life. I have had Ron for eighteen years—I've never watched football with him or talked football with him, or had to. To his credit, he never inflicts it on me. He believes there's life after football, and he loves meeting other people who are doing other things and finding out about that.

He's coaching the Sydney Swans for two and a half years. He checked with me to see if I could run the pub single-handedly; I gave him my assurance that I could. I'm finding it's becoming easier every day under the management of a woman. I've simplified systems, I put things back where I found them. The staff would go to the wall for me, the accountant is very impressed and it is now time to get back to the part-time job that I know my life should be about. I've done a painting and I feel like I'm beginning the rest of my life on my own terms again.

I don't trust men. Not at all. I have to second-think Ron every moment of his life. It doesn't keep me on my toes; it keeps him on his toes. I am already on my toes.

In company, if we had a dinner party and Ron started espousing something that I found appalling, then I'd have to dig in and say—not in a bullying way—'I just have to say if you knew more about it, Ron, you certainly wouldn't say that.' It would start like that. Being a competitive Italian type, he would wave his arms around a lot and become a debater rather than a thinker. He wants to win; he doesn't want to learn.

He grew up with the hero notion of himself on the Saturday matinees and the war hero father who died when he was three. He used to walk to school every morning along an avenue of honour of trees. So he grew up with this hero notion of his father and himself. He pitted himself against everything all his life and I find that very heartening and endearing. He is incredibly generous and kind, given half a chance.

I still don't own anything, at this moment in my life. I have no debts, I own nothing. I don't think there's anything in writing that makes me a secure person at all, but that doesn't worry me. I can always survive, and I like it that way. I'm going to look life in the gall-bladder and find it an interesting experience. I don't think you always have to have a smile on your face to be having an interesting experience.

I slackened off for a couple of years. I saw a lot of friends, I had a lot of conversations, I read a lot, I developed a lot of ideas and I did quite a bit of changing. I think I was probably really finally recuperating after the death of my father and my dearest friend. I re-established myself, and it was a very valuable time to me. A lot of people said to me, 'What are you doing?' and I said, 'I'm having a terrific time.'

Kafka probably changed my life more than any other author, because he lets you look into the big black hole. I learned something that is now standing me in good stead. There are depressed people and people who have the courage to bypass depression; I have developed that in my cartooning. I am very proud of the few cartoons that I've eventually brought to fruition because I think they are the best I've ever seen.

I began to appreciate the artists who had been through the war, who had found the courage to send themselves up, be brave and remember their humanity without whingeing. I have to say the Jews are my most and least favourite people. The Jewish shopkeeper mentality, the whingeing, self-involved boring farts that run shops are my least favourite human beings and the Jewish intellectual is probably my most favourite.

I'd go to the wall for equal rights, so I suppose Ron associates that with being a Commie. I think it goes hand in hand for him, that to be any kind of a socialist is to be a poofter. Also because, like any old hag, I have fag friends, and you know the hag needs a fag. I don't think he had encountered much of the gay community before he had met me and through the arts communities he's met a lot.

I am just myself with Ron and he's quite used to me. He takes it all in good grace and thinks that's how I am.

I am clearly a heterosexual. I have had very close relationships with women, I have lived with gay women, but unless I want to have children why would I care what sex any animal is? I don't think of anyone's age or sex, really, when I meet them. I've said to my non-biological children, 'Leave all your options open if you are going through a bit of a phase which might have headed that way. Don't decide to call yourself anything because you are just closing doors.'

Ron's a very involving person and he couldn't have stayed on the rails without terrific people like me and a secretary that he, through his own serendipity, found. She is possibly my dearest friend, equally devoted to him, and sees him without any rose-coloured glasses. It's his charisma. I never deny that. Whenever we are doing an eyeball-to-eyeball confrontation I say, 'You are simply blessed to have this unconditional support from people who know how neglectful you are, how unrepentant you are. Good for you, in the end, just good for you. If you can do it, do it.'

In my own life I am living quite separately exactly as I wish. In Ron's life I am behind him in the dust with the animals and the children and carrying all the chattels. I always have had my own life and always will have.

I was asked in a television interview last week whether I had any advice for another young sportsman's wife and I said, 'Independence, independence, independence, and value your family and friends. Create your own support group. Only be with people who do you good and can understand your form of communication.'

Ron went into a partnership with a football player called Adrian Gallagher in this hotel fourteen years ago or something, and it wasn't until two years ago that we came in to see how it was going, realised it was going very badly and decided to get in and run it ourselves. I thought I had died and gone to hell. Between us we have been doing at least 170 hours a week, so one of us had to go to Sydney. The one thing I never wanted to do was work with him. Suddenly I was drafted. We had no choice; we had to get in and clean this place up and get it back on its feet. I could see that was the reality, so I'm not going to be whingeing or bleating about it, but I have never done anything as hard or as against my principles. I am not soft, but I can't support things I don't believe in. It really hurts because I was supporting things I did not believe in, like drunkenness and bad behaviour and chauvinism.

I have always told bad patrons off, and that's why I have attracted such a good staff and finally good customers who don't mind me doing that. People come in and say 'The customer is always right' and I say, 'We don't believe in that. We wish you were right, but you're proven not to be right.'

When people do me down, I am so upfront it's unbelievable. I say things to people in the bar that bring the staff to their knees, bring Ron to his knees. He just cringes and goes away. If they're belching, farting and scratching their balls they say, 'It's just a pub.' I say, 'No, it's not just a pub. Are you married?' and if they say no, I say, 'Good. Just have an instant vasectomy. Don't get married. Don't come back here again.' I don't give a shit what they think.

I had to throw ten people out recently, a bunch of guys who were behaving appallingly. One of them said, 'Well, you can't throw all of us out' and I said, 'Yes, I can,' and I didn't know how I was going to do it but I was going to. I just won't have sub-behaviour. I think it's part of my responsibility to maintain a standard. There's Sybil Fawlty and me; we are a bit different but with the same ideals. Basil's in Sydney.

I will have just talked some drunk out the door of the hotel and Ron will arrive and say, 'G'day, mate, leaving already?' and bring him back in and show him the sports bar or show him around. I just stand there hitting my head against the wall, and so do the staff, but on the other hand we love him and miss him and think he's terrific in his own mad way.

We have had no injuries since he's left, and no breakages. He's not a team man, he's a captain coach, so he gets behind the bar, pours drinks with a deliberate kind of attitude and he broke our barman's ribs slamming open the fridge door. He rebroke them two weeks later, with the same absolute lack of awareness for anyone within the environment. He just hip-and-shoulders his way through to get it done. You either respect what he's doing or you kill him; it does boil down to that.

I have contemplated killing him many, many times. I think that's the only reason he's never physically assaulted me, because he knows it would be to the death and I might win. I can see that there's a frustration that builds up in him when his will is opposed; it's a fine line to taking it to the physical.

I haven't had an official job but I've done a lot of freelance art work in that time. I have done cartooning, brochures and textile design, which I enjoyed very much because that had a deadline involved. I'd have to work all night to do designs for Target or Venture or there might be a silk print for Georges in amongst it. An incredible range of challenging drawing assignments. I think I have enjoyed that more than any art I have ever done because of the disciplines involved in textile design. You are working to a brief and a palette. When it's seven o'clock in the morning and the sun comes up and you've done five designs and they sell at $35 000 apiece, then look at them and think, 'That's very professional work.'

I have done my best painting in two years this week. I finished it two days ago. It's a neo-Nazi dove of peace and it's eight foot by seven foot and I'm very, very pleased with it. I have hung it on my dining room wall.

I am an artist because I see like an artist and that is the joy of having a developed sense of eye, where for music lovers it's a developed sense of ear. Whether you ever put brush to canvas again you are still an artist, simply because of your perception.

My retirement plan is to run a bar for ageing eccentrics in Queensland. I'll charge the locals $300 a drink, cold water huts for the elite, a deep waters port so that I can get some international travellers and I will run it like something out of a Somerset Maugham novel. I find just sticking to your guns as good as money in a way.

All of my women friends are quite keen on my idea of a colony where we each have a little house just out of view of each, a communal bar and eating area, a library, a pool table if we're up to it. I don't want to live with boring old people; I want to live with like-minded friends.

My old age doesn't involve men, and that's just occurred naturally. It's not about being a lesbian, in spite of Ron calling me 'Commie poofter'. It's just that like-minded people tend to be women. Ron says, 'You're a man hater,' and I say, 'Yes I am, but it's not their fault or mine. If they lift their game I am very happy to reassess it.'

Just as I was about to leap into a cab, Cherryl grabbed me by the arm.

'Don't forget to emphasise my commitment to population control. I really mean what I say. What the Pope is doing and saying, especially for Third World people, is wicked. When you hear he's been stabbed with an AIDS-infected needle, look for me in the Bahamas. See you later. Bye!'

Now there's a woman who knows how to hold your attention right to the end.